D1649033

TEMPT-AWAY

First read

How to Defeat Temptation in Under 60 Seconds

And How to Recover Quickly When You Don't

TEMPT-AWAY

Guy Hammond

TEMPT-AWAY: *How to Defeat Temptation in Under 60 Seconds*
© 2015 by Guy Hammond

Printed in the United States of America.

ISBN: 978-1-941988-14-5.

Unless otherwise indicated, all Scripture references are from the *Holy Bible, New International Version*, copyright 1973, 1978, 1984, 2011 by the International Bible Society. Used by permission.

Passages marked NLT are from the *Holy Bible, New Living Translation* copyright © 1996, 2004, 2007 by Tyndale House Foundation. Used by permission of Tyndale House Publishers Inc., Carol Stream, Illinois 60188. All rights reserved. New Living, NLT, and the New Living Translation logo are registered trademarks of Tyndale House Publishers.

Cover design by Roy Appalsamy of AMDesign, Inc.

Interior design by Toney Mulhollan. Text is set using Constantia and Trade Gothic Standard.

Copy editor: Amy Morgan and Illumination Publishers.

Illumination Publishers is committed to caring wisely for God's creation and uses recycled paper whenever possible.

About the author: Before becoming a Christian in 1987, Guy lived the life of an active homosexual for over a decade. Today he is the Executive  Director of Strength in Weakness Ministries, educating Christians on the complex and hot button issues surrounding homosexuality and same-sex attractions. He has taught tens of thousands of people through his workshops all over the world. He has been married for twenty-five years to his wife Cathy, and they have four children. They make their home near Toronto, Ontario, Canada.

ILLUMINATION
PUBLISHERS

www.ipibooks.com
6010 Pinecreek Ridge Court
Spring, Texas 77379-2513

Contents

Acknowledgements

My wife, Cathy, and I have been on this journey together for twenty-five years. How can I thank you enough, honey, for believing in me when I often didn't believe in myself? You are the absolute love and joy of my life, the greatest gift God has ever given me. I will truly cherish you until my dying breath.

My four amazing children have been on this journey too, but they didn't have a choice—sorry about that, guys! I am aware that it's not easy for you to have a father who is same-sex attracted. Thank you for loving your dad unconditionally and not allowing this weakness to diminish me in your eyes. You can't possibly understand how much I love you and how grateful I am to have you in my life.

My parents and my siblings are obviously a huge part of my story. Thank you for being so patient and understanding with me as I strive to figure out this part of my life.

My closest advisors and trusted lifelong friends, Mike and Barb Lock, Andrew and Suzette Lewis, Dave and Rejane Burrage, Neil D'Souza, and Sheridan and Debbie Wright, thank you for all you have done for the Hammond family.

My Advisory Board for Strength in Weakness Ministries has been so helpful. Thank you for your willingness to associate your esteemed names and reputations with this sometimes fragile and outside-the-box ministry! Dr. Douglas Jacoby, Andrew Lewis and Dr. F. LaGard Smith, I am incredibly grateful for the kindness you have shown me.

My support staff at Strength in Weakness Ministries has helped to make my dream come true in establishing a ministry that assists same-sex-attracted Christians all over the world. None of this would have been possible without you. Thank you, Kris and Nicole Boyer, Jaco and Pat Ferreira, Kathy MacBrien, Stephen and Deb Bowen, Brandon Redler, Mike Yager and Morgan Roberts for your continued involvement.

Introduction

Cheap Infomercial or the Real Deal?

There are worse things in life than death. If you've ever spent an evening with an insurance sales-man, you know exactly what I mean. —Woody Allen

It's 3:30 a.m. and you're exhausted beyond belief, but no matter how hard you try, you just can't sleep. The alarm on your smartphone will start buzzing in a few short hours announcing the start of a new day, and it's going to be a long and busy one. You've tried everything you know to doze off and hopefully dream your way into a coma, but absolutely nothing has worked. You've turned down the temperature, readjusted your pillow into every possible configuration, imagined being at your favorite place on earth, counted sheep, put a pillow between your thighs, meditated, taken melatonin, had milk and Oreos, read something boring (hopefully that is not why you are reading this right now), taken a hot shower, listened to a sleep hypnosis podcast, rubbed your belly for comfort, only to find yourself still wide awake.

Totally frustrated, you lumber awkwardly out of your bedroom and out to the couch and plop yourself down with TV remote in hand. With over 800 channels to choose from, surely there must be something worth watching; but of course, there is not. Reruns, music videos and documentaries. You finally run into a series of infomercials: what are these guys trying to sell now? You flip from one cheesy sales pitch to another: the Chillow Pillow that turns your pillow into a "chillow" (Oh, man! I don't have a Chillow! No wonder I can't sleep!). The Snuggie—the blanket with sleeves. Spray-on hair—remove that ugly bald spot! The Chop-O-Matic—chop, mince, cube, slice and dice anything in seconds! The Clapper—clap on, clap off. On the next channel that old lady has fallen again, and she still can't get up! Would SOMEBODY please help the poor woman? Where is her family, for cryin' out loud! Oh look, there's the ShamWow guy. You'll be saying, "Wow!" every time you need a towel. Doesn't drip, doesn't make a mess, great for home, the boat and the RV! Hey, I just yawned; that's a good sign!

You're just about to give up and turn off the tube and try to sleep again, but the next infomercial is like an accident you can't not watch; you're glued. It's the Night Glow Seat, the toilet seat that glows neon blue, for only $69.99. Whoa! $69.99 for a glow-in-the-dark toilet seat? You've got to be kidding me. Who on earth would be dumb enough to buy a toilet seat that glows in the dark? Suddenly, memories of that cute but annoying little saying that your mother hung above the toilet when you were young comes back to you: "If you sprinkle when you tinkle, be a sweetie and wipe the seatie." Maybe $69.99 is worth it after all, especially since you can do it in three easy payments. Mom would be so proud. You jump up excitedly to grab your credit card, thinking of all the ways your life (and anyone else's who will ever use your toilet at night) is about to change forever, but before you can get the number to call, the infomercial abruptly ends, the next one jumps on, and a booming voice announces:

> Introducing the incredible, all new, never-before-offered product that no Christian can live without! Has it been difficult for you to overcome temptation? Do you find yourself tired of struggling through your Christian life, having to deal with the same areas of sinful enticement, over and over again? Do you find yourself quickly and easily succumbing to the daily temptations you face, with little or no resistance at all? Do you feel trapped, unable to overcome your fascination with worldly pleasures? Have you wondered if you've

got the strength to carry on?

What if you could quickly and successfully crush and overpower every temptation you face, all within seconds? **That's right, just seconds!** Now you can defeat each and every sinful seduction that comes your way in less time than it takes to watch this commercial. Get ready for *Tempt-Away*, the revolutionary, simple, four-point plan that will help you wipe out and annihilate all of the temptations you experience, without exception. When tempted, just apply the first *Tempt-Away* step. If the temptation persists, administer each *Tempt-Away* temptation-busting step as needed, and you'll discover that the temptation will disappear, often within thirty to sixty seconds!

And there's nothing like *Tempt-Away* for those special times like the holidays, on hot sunny days at the beach, at tax time or when you find yourself away from your Christian friends. Lust, fantasy, impurity, gossip, deceit, slander, anger, selfishness and more will be zapped away in significantly less time that it will take to hear a sermon!

The *secret is in the unique four-point success strategy that Tempt-Away* creator Guy Hammond has personally used for years with tremendous success, combined with spiritual truths found only in the Bible. With *Tempt-Away* you're always ready for Satan's attack. You could pay thousands of dollars to go to workshops and classes and buy workbooks galore, but you can get this revolutionary, one of a kind, simple, four-point plan to overcome every temptation you face for one low price if you click or call right away.

But wait, that's not all! We're not stopping there! As part of the *Tempt-Away* "buy-it-today" special offer, we're going to give you something else you can't do without! Yes, this is one temptation no one can resist! Other than Jesus, no one has ever lived a perfect life, and as amazing as *Tempt-Away* is, there will be times when you will still decide to sin. Order *Tempt-Away* right now and we'll add Guy Hammond's exclusive and unique game plan on how to quickly recover from any sin committed. That's two, yes, two **Tempt-Away** products for the price of one! And every **Tempt-Away** package comes with a guarantee: simply follow the four simple steps faithfully, and you will lose those unwanted sins fast! Don't wait, call 1-888-TEMPT-AWAY now! Or go to temptaway. org... That's 1-888-TEMPT-AWAY or temptaway.org. Operators are standing by!

You quickly call the one-triple-eight number and order Tempt-Away, and after hanging up, the desire for sleep finally washes over you. You realize it was a guilty conscience that was keeping you up all night, but now that Tempt-Away is on its way, you feel empowered, ready to implement this new, breakthrough system; it's just what you needed! Quickly you fall into a deep and peaceful sleep.

My Confession

> *No temptation has overtaken you except what is common to mankind. And God is faithful; he will not let you be tempted beyond what you can bear. But when you are tempted, he will also provide a way out so that you can endure it.* (1 Corinthians 10:13)

As of the writing of this chapter (July 2015), I have been a Christian for twenty-seven years and eleven months. (Yes, I count the months; every month that passes I'm one month closer to eternity!) I wish I could tell you how easy I find it to live a sinless life, but the truth is that most days are difficult and challenging in this regard. Most days, I find myself in the midst of a spiritual battle to do what is right, although it's true that the longer I have been a Christian and the more I employ the steps to overcome temptation as advertised in this book (cleverly packaged as Tempt-Away), the more I enjoy hours and hours of victory surrounding those few weak moments. I have dedicated a lot of years and energy to trying to be a godly man, to obey the Scriptures and to live as God has asked me to, but in spite of the promise of 1 Corinthians 10:13, regardless of my best efforts I fail, and sometimes miserably. The whole process shows me the frailty of my life and how weak I truly am. Thank God for his grace and mercy! Praise God that it is impossible to "out sin" God's love and forgiveness.

Does Tempt-Away Actually Work?

So what about this Tempt-Away plan? Does it actually work, or am I just a cheap infomercial salesman hawking my own cheesy product? Well, I grant you that packaging these four biblical principles together as Tempt-Away might be a little cheesy (I had to call it something!), but the claims are real. I promise you, if you faithfully and consistently follow the four-step protocol that I offer in this book whenever you are tempted to sin, regardless of the type of temptation you face, you will find that the number of times you give in when enticed to sin will drop dramatically and your level of personal righteousness will skyrocket to new heights. This program will work no matter where you are in your spiritual journey right now, whether you've been a Christian for thirty minutes or thirty years, whether you have the role of elder, pastor or evangelist or can barely find your way to church on Sunday mornings.

To top all that, this book will explain this four-point game plan, my reasoning behind it and the biblical teachings to back it all up, along with some great tips to help you be successful. You will find that in real time you are able to actually implement as many of the four steps as you need in order to overcome temptation, most often within thirty to sixty seconds, meaning that this is a method you can successfully put into practice as many times as you need to, all through the day and night, no matter where you are or what you are doing. Whether you're at home, work or school, on the bus, driving your car or walking down the street, at a sporting event or lying on the beach, sitting in church or plopped down on the sofa watching infomercials, you can do this. It's a plan I have followed for years and it has benefited my life tremendously.

This probably leaves you asking an obvious question: if Tempt-Away works so well, what's with the seemingly contradictory confession that I'm such a sinner? Fair question. My answer: welcome to the broken, human condition. Romans 3:23 states that "all have sinned and fallen short of the glory of God." 1 John 1:8 (KJV) says, "If we say that we have no sin, we deceive ourselves, and the truth is not in us." There is no way I would even think of claiming to be sinless because

I have this nifty four-point plan to overcome every temptation. Is the problem with the plan or with me? Well, since the four-point plan is based on biblical principles and works when used, clearly the problem is with me. I humbly and awkwardly concede that I sometimes fail at following my own advice. I embarrassingly admit that there are times when I want to sin more than I want to be obedient to God. But hey, I'm in good company; Paul wrote:

> *I have the desire to do what is good, but I cannot carry it out. For I do not do the good I want to do, but the evil I do not want to do—this I keep on doing.* (Romans 7:18b–19)

So when I do sin, it's not because the plan doesn't work; it's because I purposely chose not to be righteous and follow the plan. When I do, I overcome temptation. When I don't, more often than not, I fail.

You've Got to Love Being Needy

Several years ago I attended a meeting that was being hosted by a local church for those who struggle with all kinds of addiction; mostly alcohol, drug and sex addiction. I was on the verge of beginning my *Strength in Weakness* website and knew that there would be occasions when those who suffered sexual addiction in its various forms would reach out for help through our ministry. I thought that attending this class would provide some needed training and education for me.

The event took place in a somewhat seedy part of town, and I remember that when I entered the room I was struck by how disheveled most of the people looked. Clearly the majority of these poor folks suffered with a lot of problems and issues. Sitting in the back and scanning the audience I remember thinking to myself, "Wow, these people are really needy." This incredibly self-righteous, pompous and smug attitude continued on for quite a while, much to my shame. Then suddenly it hit me (or shall I say God gave me a serious spiritual slap upside the head) that I am needy too! How dare I sit in judgment of any of these people? In fact, these individuals were heroes for having the courage to admit that they had problems to work through, and they were smart and humble enough to know they needed help to do it. I'm embarrassed for the sinful thoughts I had that day towards everyone else in that room.

You have to love being needy. If you're not needy, you don't need Jesus. He didn't come for those who have it all together; no, he came for those who don't have it all together. Being needy is not normally considered a positive thing, is it? I mean, who would want to be friends with a "needy" person. "Hello, my name is Guy, I'm really needy. Do you want to be my friend?" Introduce yourself with that line and you'll be lonelier than a Monday morning church building for a long time. But Jesus loves needy people.

I don't know who to credit with this thought, but I like it: "Never trust a Christian who walks without a limp." In my many years of Christianity, I've seen a lot of people act like their lives are perfect. They don't want anyone to see them limp. I don't understand Christians like that. Their marriages are perfect, their kids are perfect, their finances are perfect, their houses are perfect, their hair is perfect. They rarely, if ever, confess sin or weakness although often their broken areas are plain for everyone else to see. I don't get it. Do they think that the rest of us would be surprised to find out they're sinners? We already know that. Do they think it would somehow be a shock to God and the angels that they are broken, sinful people? Why is it that some try to hide the fact that they are in need? Jesus said in Luke 5:31 (ESV) that "those who are well have no need of a physician, but those who are sick." If you're not sick, if you're not broken, if you're not needy, then don't bother with Jesus, because you've apparently figured it out on your own.

Why I Need Jesus the Physician

In order for you to understand my perspective on the issues we're discussing, you need to know a little of who I am. I have been married for twenty-four years to the love of my life, have four amazing children, and have been an evangelist and counsellor since the late 1990s. I am also same-gender attracted. Before becoming a Christian in 1987 I lived an actively gay life for over ten years. During that time I had a boyfriend for several years and was sexually involved with many different partners. By the time I was in my early twenties, I was spent. Over a decade of hiding in plain sight, afraid to be real with the people I loved the most, terrified of rejection if they knew who I really was, clandestine and anonymous sexual encounters and the breakup of a relationship with my boyfriend of many years had taken its toll. In God's perfect timing, he sent someone to invite me to church.

Having grown up in a church environment, I was skeptical, doubting that any pragmatic help would be found there, but I was wrong. It took two years of going to church, hearing the Word and trying to figure things out, but finally I was ready to turn my life over to God. I became a Christian on August 15, 1987 and can tell you that I have not participated in any kind of homosexual activity since my conversion almost twenty-eight years ago.

God Is Mysterious to Me

God is mysterious to me; I don't know why he works the way he does, and if I were God I might do things differently. But the truth of Guy Hammond is that in spite of thousands of hours of prayer and study and begging and crying and marriage and having kids and doing full-time ministry, and trying to figure this out, my attraction to the same gender has not diminished. I am just as attracted to the same sex today as the day I gave my life to Christ. Over and over again the Lord has lovingly told me, "Guy, don't worry about this. I love you. 'My grace is sufficient for you, for my power is made perfect in weakness'" (2 Corinthians 12:9).

And so God has worked miraculously over the years to bless me with a wife and children, with going into the full-time ministry, and now to create and oversee an international ministry that helps thousands around the world (*Strength in Weakness Ministries*). While not the focus of this particular book, if you're interested in knowing how to share your faith with gays and lesbians in your community in a loving and respectful way that does not lower the biblical sexual ethic, if you want to learn how to encourage and support same-sex-attracted Christians, if you're interested in knowing how to best deal with the gay rights movement, then you've got to purchase my first book *Caring Beyond the Margins: What Every Christian Needs to Know About Homosexuality.*[1]

I wanted to share with you a small piece of my personal story here because I will refer to the challenges I face as a homosexually attracted Christian throughout these pages. I believe that having to bow this area of weakness to God's will (not always an easy thing to do) has given me unique perspective on what it means to overcome the daily temptations and yearnings we all experience, regardless of what form they come in. I want you to know that this book comes from the life of a man who does not have it all together, who has fallen many times and who is indeed needy but continues to rise and who refuses to quit, and from someone who has successfully put together a neat little plan that when used, really does work.

So you're about to spend the next several hours with a salesman, and I trust that by the time we're done, you won't feel the same way Woody Allen does about hucksters like me, because I'm about to reveal to you a product that really will impact your life for the good; yes, even better than the Clapper, ShamWow and the world famous Night Glow Seat for $69.99. Just read the book, do your best to follow the steps provided, and experience newfound freedom over sin. Are you ready? Welcome to Tempt-Away.

End Note:_____
1. Available from www.ipibooks.com.

Chapter One

Redefining Temptation

I've missed more than 9,000 shots in my career. I've lost almost 300 games. Twenty-six times I've been trusted to take the game-winning shot and missed. I've failed over and over and over again in my life. And that is why I succeed. —Michael Jordan

When writing a book, I figure people should stick with what they know, with what they've been successful at in life. I mean, if someone is going to ask me to shell out hard-earned cash and then actually expect me to read the thing, they better know what they're talking about, right? Who, for instance, would ever buy *How to Love Your Enemies* by Osama Bin Laden, or *Why* The Interview *Is My Favorite Movie* by Kim Jong-un? How about *How to Sing Opera* by Justin Bieber or *How to Lose Weight and Keep It Off* by, well...me? Exactly. Colossal flops before they're published. Why? Seal Team Six took out Osama for a reason. Kim Jong-un so feared the release of Seth Rogen's American political comedy portraying an attempt on his life that the Democratic People's Republic of North Korea "covertly" hacked SONY's computer systems and then threatened mass terrorism should the spoof ever make it to the big screen. In my opinion, the little dictator made much ado about nothing, considering that *The Interview* made the

Police Academy movies look like *Masterpiece Theatre*. As for Justin Bieber, well, in my humble estimation, the poor guy can barely sing pop, his genre of choice, much less anything else, regardless of what *Tiger Beat* magazine and 50 million googly eyed teenybop girls say.

And then there's the book I'm holding off on writing on weight loss; I did join a gym last year, spent four hundred bucks; haven't lost a pound. Apparently you have to go there. Besides, I read that the average human heart will beat 2.5 billion times in a lifetime. Your heart has only so many beats, and then that's it, so I figure I shouldn't waste those heartbeats on exercise, because everything wears out eventually. Speeding up your heart will not make you live longer; that's like saying you can extend the life of your car by driving it faster.[1] The way I figure it is, if you want to live longer, sit on the couch and watch a show and slow things down; save those heartbeats! Of course, I have no scientific proof to back this up and I've struggled with my weight by whole life...maybe I should rethink that one.

On the other hand, if you want to know the secret on how to hit home runs, I suggest you read *I Had a Hammer* by the man who has been named the Home Run King, Hank Aaron. (Only Barry Bonds had more dingers, but for baseball purists, he doesn't count due to the use of illegal steroids.) Ole Hank touched 'em all a whopping 755 times in his twenty-three-year career, passing Ruth and Willie Mays.

If you ever want to know how to invest like Buffett, you can't improve on the bestselling collection of Warren's letters to Berkshire Hathaway shareholders, *The Essays of Warren Buffett*. I mean, how can you argue with the wealthiest venture capitalist on earth, one whose net worth hovers around the 70- to 80-billion-dollar mark? If you want to delve into the psyche of one of the greatest jocks in history to learn what drove him to the pinnacle of his sport, then get a copy of *I Can't Accept Not Trying* by Michael Jordan. If French cuisine best suits your palate, you can't improve on Julia Child's 1961 classic cookbook *Mastering the Art of French Cooking*. Worldwide bestsellers, all of them. Why? They lived it. No hypocrisy, no bull; they're the real deal and they've got the stats to prove it.

Welcome to the dilemma we face with this book. I say "we" because if you are reading this, it means we're in this together. I'm the bold proclaimer with the audacity to write a book promising to reveal to you a simple strategy that if employed will guarantee that your ability to overcome and defeat *every* temptation you face will dramatically increase, and you're the one left hoping that I'm not like Justin Bieber teaching you how to sing opera. So the question begs to be asked: am I the real deal with the stats to prove it, or is my game plan (cleverly branded as Tempt-Away) just a cheap cure-all, a spiritual panacea?

Will You Give Me the Same Leeway as Hammerin' Hank?

Well, actually, yes, I do know what I'm talking about. I've lived it. No bull; I am the real deal; I'm not wasting your time; I do actually have a strategy that I have used for years that has significantly improved my ability to overcome the enticement to sin and most often do it in under sixty seconds. As clearly stated in the introduction, I've not done any of this perfectly, of course, but there is no doubt that whenever I have engaged these four steps at the moment that temptation enters my consciousness, my success rate at overcoming that temptation has dramatically increased. All I ask, in measuring my definition of success, is that you afford me the same kind of leeway that everyone freely gives Hank Aaron, Warren Buffett, Michael Jordan and Julia Child.

Hammerin' Hank, as he was nicknamed, hit 755 fast balls over the fence, that's true, but had 12,364 at bats to accomplish that remarkable feat and ended his career with a .305 batting average, which means that he hit the ball only thirty percent of the time, meaning, of course, that seventy percent of the time, he failed. And what of Mr. Buffett? In 1989 the then forty-nine-year-old Chairman of the Board wrote a letter to Berkshire Hathaway shareholders conceding all of the mistakes he had made and the lessons learned from them the previous year. Michael Jordan's humble confession of repeated failure that is displayed at the beginning of this chapter says it all, doesn't it? Over 9,000 missed shots! And what of Julia Child? She may be known as one of the greatest culinary artists and gourmet chefs in history, but even she had to divulge, "One of the secrets, and pleasures, of cooking is to learn to correct something if it goes awry; and one of the lessons is to grin and bear it if it cannot be fixed."

So, let me ask, is the Home Run King a failure for not hitting the ball seventy percent of the time? Cooperstown and history say no; in fact they say he's one of the greatest of all time for getting it right only thirty percent of the time. Is Michael Jordan a lousy basketball player because, as he said, he "failed over and over and over again"? Is Buffett to be considered a loser, a man whose advice is not worth listening to, because he confessed to making several regrettable mistakes? Should we ignore the culinary genius of Julia Child because she overcooked her baguettes every now and then? Obviously not.

So as we proceed together and I share my personal game plan for victory over temptation, let me ask: Would you be happy to know that I have the same stats as Hank Aaron, that I overcome thirty percent of the temptations I face, meaning that I sin seventy percent of the time? Would those numbers be good enough to put me in the church's "Hall of Fame," or would I be considered a failure as a Christian, leaving you to suddenly ship this book back demanding a refund? Well, if thirty percent isn't good enough, what is? Fifty, seventy-five, ninety or one hundred percent?

Should Paul Be in the Spiritual Hall of Fame?

Back to the apostle Paul, whom we briefly quoted in the introduction. Will you give me the same leeway you are willing to give him? Would you be happy to know that my "stats" in overcoming the temptation to sin are equal to his? What will we do with a man who wrote the majority of the New Testament and yet said of his daily struggle to overcome temptation:

> I do not understand what I do. For what I want to do I do not do, but what I hate I do. And if I do what I do not want to do, I agree that the law is good. As it is, it is no longer I myself who do it, but it is sin living in me. For I know that good itself does not dwell in me, that is, in my sinful nature. For I have the desire to do what is good, but I cannot carry it out. For I do not do the good I want to do, but the evil I do not want to do—this I keep on doing. Now if I do what I do not want to do, it is no longer I who do it, but it is sin living in me that does it.
>
> So I find this law at work: Although I want to do good, evil is right there with me. For in my inner being I delight in God's law; but I see another law at work in me, waging war against the law of my mind and making me a prisoner of the law of sin at work within me. What a wretched man I am! (Romans 7:15–24)

Hardly sounds like Hall of Fame material, does it? With this passage we find some of the most brutally honest and heartfelt words penned by any man and, I must say, one of the most moving passages in Scripture, because here Paul is giving us his own spiritual autobiography and laying bare his very heart and soul.

Here Paul deals with the torturing paradox of God's laws. In themselves, God's laws are holy; they come from a sphere other than this world. God's laws are divine; we have in them the very voice of God. And so we see here a man who is baring his very soul, and he is telling us of an experience that we can all relate to, one that speaks of the very essence of the human condition. Paul knew what was right and wanted to do what was right, and yet, somehow, he kept doing what was wrong. Paul knew what was wrong and the last thing he wanted to do was to do it, and yet, somehow, he did it. Did he not have the ability, the capability to overcome every temptation he faced? Certainly he did; hence the dilemma he faced. In a twist of spiritual irony, it is Paul himself, this imperfect man who struggled to do what is right, who also told us how possible it is to overcome every temptation we face:

> So, if you think you are standing firm, be careful that you don't fall! No temptation has overtaken you except what is common to mankind. And God is faithful; he will not let you be tempted beyond what you can bear. But when you are tempted, he will also provide a way out so that you can endure it.
> (1 Corinthians 10:12–13)

Clearly, knowing what to do, having the capability to do it and actually doing it are not the same! Whenever I read that scripture I can so relate to the pain that Paul felt.

Why We Must Embrace Failure

I have a critical point to stress that may seem inconsistent on the surface with the whole purpose of this book, but it is not, and I'll explain. The goal of our lives as Christians *should not* be to stop sinning. I don't think Paul spent his entire time trying not to sin; I think he spent his life trying to serve and glorify God. Focusing on personal righteousness is certainly a part of that picture, but if your measure of success as a Christian and your feeling of closeness to God is determined on how righteous or sinful you have been in the last twenty-four-hour period, then you've got to get off that treadmill as fast as you can; perfection this side of heaven is an impossible pursuit. No one will ever or has ever lived a sinless life, except Christ, and you aren't him!

If you're one of those poor souls who is hardwired to be a perfectionist (it's not my gig, but many are) and you have transferred that expectation from your professional life or educational pursuits into your Christian walk, you're not only in for a long and disappointing journey, but living your spiritual life with that self-imposed expectation isn't even biblical. It's faulty theology. Strive for perfection at school and get straight As, or in other pursuits in life, sure, knock yourself out, but when it comes to the Christian walk, it is not God's expectation that you live a sinless life; that plan was squashed in Eden. If the Lord expected us to live sinless lives and knew that we had the potential to accomplish it, sending his Son to die for our sins would have been completely unnecessary. So failure is not an option, it is a requirement! Can you handle that truth?

Chapter Eight of this book ("It's All in How You Bounce") will help you learn how to deal with the inevitable: that regardless of your best efforts and purest motivations, you will sin, you will fail and in fact, you need to fail, or you'll never be able to be one with Christ.

The inescapable reality that we will sin, however, does not take away our responsibility to try our best; it is up to us to keep moving forward, to try to improve and do better, to progress closer and closer to Christlikeness, which is perfection. Just because perfection is unattainable doesn't mean we don't endeavor to improve.

Temptation Has Gotten a Bad Rap

Temptation, I think, has gotten a bad rap because many Christians misunderstand how God feels about temptation and how he uses it to the betterment of our spiritual well-being. Many of us desperately need to experience a total paradigm shift on the issue of temptation. I want to challenge you to look at this topic through a new set of lenses. Doing so is a key component of my Tempt-Away game plan.

While it is true that Satan is the one doing the tempting, or takes advantage of our evil inner desires to sin, what the devil intends for evil and chaos in our lives, God actually turns into good, in the form of opportunities for us to honor him and grow spiritually. We all face many different kinds of trials in our lives: financial trials, health trials, exam trials, children trials, parent trials, employment trials; but certainly one of the most consistent and severe spiritual trials that we face daily are the trials of temptation.

James chapter 1 goes into depth on the issue of trials and temptations that would be foolish for us to ignore. As we look at this chapter, it appears on the surface that James is having a hard time focusing, as if he's almost in a state of dementia, haphazardly and quickly shifting from subject to subject that are independent of one another, yet in reality these thoughts are intricately linked in such a manner that explains temptation and trials in a way not found anywhere else in Scripture. Stay with me and let's unpack this together.

The author of James (widely presumed to be James the brother of Jesus) launches into his epistle to the Jews scattered among the nations by talking about trials in chapter 1 verse 2: "Consider it pure joy, my brothers and sisters, whenever you face trials of many kinds, because you know that the testing of your faith produces perseverance." He then shifts to prayer in verses 5 to 8: "If any of you lacks wisdom, you should ask God, who gives generously to all without finding fault, and it will be given to you..." He then suddenly moves on to discussing the plight of the wealthy and the poor in verses 9 to 11: "Believers in humble circumstances ought to take pride in their high position. But the rich should take pride in their humiliation—since they will pass away like a wild flower..." Then the author goes back to the topic that he started with, trials: "Blessed is the one who perseveres under trial because, having stood the test, that person will receive the crown of life that the Lord has promised to those who love him." He then moves over to discussing temptation in verses 13 and 14:

When tempted, no one should say, "God is tempting me." For God cannot be tempted by evil, nor does he tempt anyone; but each person is tempted when they are dragged away by their own evil desire and enticed. Then, after desire has conceived, it gives birth to sin; and sin, when it is full-grown, gives birth to death.

And then he finishes off with a brief teaching on understanding the gifts of God in verses 16 to 18: "Don't be deceived, my dear brothers and sisters. Every good and perfect gift is from above..."

The first thing this passage teaches us is that every change in our circumstance, whether considered positive or negative, offers us a test in life that we will either pass or fail. How we deal with the blessings and curses of life are all tests, opportunities for us to move closer to God or to move farther away from him. As an example, James discusses the condition of the wealthy and the poor because humans are given the opportunity to respond to poverty or wealth in either godly or ungodly ways. The poor man can either be humbly reliant on God for his daily sustenance or be bitter and angry with God that he is impoverished. The wealthy man can either be humbled by his prosperity, grateful to God for such a blessing and thereby generous to those around him because of it, or be prideful and arrogant, thinking that he is the maker of his own good fortune, hoarding the wealth for himself alone. Both circumstances are a test for either man that could be a temptation to sin.

Tim Keller does an excellent job explaining it: "Every trial is a temptation... God tests us but he never tempts us. God may give us a test, a circumstance from the outside, but if we find that that test leads us to sin, it's not God who is tempting us...the test may come from God but the temptation will come from the inside... Every adversity *and* every prosperity, every difficulty *and* every success is a test that could either make you much wiser as an opportunity for great growth, and it, if you handle it properly...will move you on toward...the crown of life. But the same opportunity is also a terrible danger and if you mishandle it, it moves you from temptation into sin and to death."[2]

Our lives are filled with good times and bad. We've all experienced the thrill of victory and the agony of defeat, both amazing blessings and incredibly difficult challenges. These are all events that present each of us with a test, and we will either persevere under the stresses we face (good or bad) and pass the test successfully, or we will give in to temptation and decide to sin. No wonder James pleads with us to turn to God in prayer, asking for wisdom as we live our lives.

As for James' alternate use of the words "trials" and "temptations," Keller points out that there is no disconnect. The very same Greek word that he uses for both is the same, which is *peirasmos*. The same word has several nuances. When it comes to trials, the nuance has to do with the inner enticement we all have towards sin.[3]

So then, how should we handle the temptations we face? Consider it pure joy! How do most of us normally handle the temptations? We hate them, we wish they weren't there, we wonder why we suffer them and even sometimes think that there must be something wrong with us that we would undergo the enticement to sin.

Being Tempted to Sin Is Not Sinful

In Matthew 4, Mark 1 and Luke 4 (for whatever reason the Holy Spirit did not move John to discuss it), the curtain is peeled back for us to see Christ in the midst of an intense time of temptation in the desert. This occurred at the beginning of his ministry. God was telling Jesus to take his love to all of mankind and to love them literally to death. Satan, on the other hand, was tempting Jesus to conquer the world through power, force and dictatorship. Time and time again, Jesus overcame. He always did, right to the end. Hebrews 4:14–16 tells us that the Lord was tempted in every way and yet did not commit a single sin. Knowing how high the stakes were, I'm sure the devil did not play around with Jesus, but rather made him the very focus of his full attention. If the devil could get Jesus to sin just one time, just once, it would be a game-changer for eternity for all of mankind. Can you imagine the attack Satan must have leveled at Christ every day for his entire adult life?

When I consider the number of temptations I face every day and how intense they sometimes can be (and I'm a nobody), I can't imagine the kind of faith, courage, self-control and reliance on God it must have taken Christ to overcome every single temptation, every minute of every day for almost two decades. Hebrews 4:15 says that Jesus was tempted in every way, just as you and I are, yet he did not sin. Of course, I don't think that means that Christ literally underwent every possible temptation known to mankind; it's a general statement helping us to understand that Christ suffered as we do.

That being said, consider the long list of temptations available to us; consider all of the temptations Christ could have experienced: to lie, cheat, steal, lust, be impure, gossip, slander, hate, lash out, fight back, be arrogant, kill, swear, falsely accuse, be bitter, be selfish, complain, tell or laugh at filthy jokes, be prejudiced, disobey his parents, get drunk, have sex with men, have sex with women, cheat on his taxes, extort, flatter for gain, be a glutton, be anxious, blaspheme, boast, envy, quarrel, covet, be greedy, mock, riot, not forgive, be ungrateful; shall we go on? No wonder angels had to attend him (Mark 1:13). No wonder we are told of several examples of him going off alone to be with his Father in prayer. No wonder we are told in that same passage in Hebrews that "we do not have a high priest who is unable to empathize with our weaknesses" and that we can "approach God's throne of grace with confidence, so that we may receive mercy and find grace to help us in our time of need." Whatever your attraction, whatever your weakness, regardless of in what form the temptation comes, Jesus has been there and has overcome.

My Self-Inflicted Wounds

Being a Christian man who lives outside the heterosexual mainstream, I can tell you how for years my shame and embarrassment over being homosexually attracted left me almost spiritually and emotionally paralyzed. This, by the way, was not anyone else's fault but my own; it was a self-inflicted wound. For the first nineteen years of my Christianity, when I was tempted to lust, I felt as guilty as if I had committed the sin, even though I had not sinned. Then of course, when I did give in to my homoerotic temptations and had a lustful thought or fantasy, or looked at a man with lust in my heart, I felt guilty too. That means that I spent the majority of my time feeling remorseful. It was an exhausting way to live, not to mention completely unbiblical.

As mentioned in the introduction, I have not participated in any kind of homosexual activity since my conversion to Christ on August 15, 1987, but the attraction has never diminished. Not only was my insecurity over that reality taken advantage of by Satan, but also my misunderstanding of the issue of temptation. And then there was the recording that was on repeat that played over and over again in my head. It was a daily routine for me to think thoughts like, "Guy, what is wrong with you that you can't change this?" "If people knew who you really are, they would never love you." "God can't love you like this." Around and around I would go, day after day, actually believing these ridiculous thoughts.

I felt like an elephant in the circus. If you've ever been to the circus you'll know that sometimes they put a 15,000-pound (7,000-kg) elephant in the ring and tie his trunk to a rope that is fixed to a stake hammered in the middle of the ring. Around and around the elephant will go, doing tricks for the audience while he walks in a never-ending circle with his trainer. It leaves you wondering, why doesn't the elephant just yank the stake out of the ground and walk out? I mean, who's going to stop a 15,000-pound beast from doing what he wants to? Why does the heaviest land animal in the world succumb to the demands of a 150-pound dude with a top hat and cane and a rope he could break in one simple yank? The reason why the elephant doesn't pull the stake out of the ground and escape is because he was trained from birth to believe that he can't, that he doesn't have the ability to pull that stake up and walk out. That of course is ridiculous, but it is what the elephant believes, and therefore he is held captive. That is how I lived until I finally realized that I didn't have to stay tied down to those negative thoughts that dominated my thinking. I decided to yank that stake of negativity out of the ground and refuse to believe it any more.

After almost twenty years of a self-inflicted sentence that left me feeling mostly lonely, isolated and in a constant state of thinking I had disappointed God, I finally decided that I was going to believe Hebrews 4:14–16 and live like I believed it. How sad—so many wasted years, so many people I could have helped, so much fear and isolation and insecurity, all because of shame and embarrassment and a paralyzing fear of what others would think of me if they knew the truth.

I finally came to an incredible revelation that shook my world; it's one that may seem obvious to you, and I probably should have caught on a lot earlier, but I'm just grateful I finally realized this truth, which is that I don't have to believe everything I think. Not every thought that comes into my mind is true. I have the ability to actually challenge the thoughts that run through my thick skull and compare them with Scripture. If the thought does not align with what I know of God, or does not sound like something God would say to me, I discard it. If the thought does align with Scripture, and it does sound like the voice of my loving Savior, I keep it and use it.

Making these changes also led me to these truths on temptation: It is not a sin to be tempted. It's not a sin to be homosexually attracted any more than it is a sin to be heterosexually attracted. An attraction is neither good nor bad; it is neutral in nature; it is just an attraction. It's what you and I decide to do with our attractions that matter. While Scripture clearly states five times, in both testaments, that actively being involved in homosexuality is not a part of God's plan for human sexuality, nowhere does Scripture teach that one must be heterosexually attracted to be a follower of Christ and go to heaven. It is my conviction that God is not concerned with who we are attracted to. For the Christian, the opposite of homosexuality is not heterosexuality; it is holiness. The goal for the same-gender-attracted follower of Christ, then, is not to try to become heterosexually attracted, but to strive to live a holy life.

Since deciding to change the way I think about temptation, I have been set free. I no longer bemoan the homoerotic temptations that I experience. No. In fact, I celebrate in them. Why? Because in them, I am able to claim the crown of life that God has promised me. I choose to take this area of weakness and the temptations I face and use them to glorify God. As for my fears of what others think of me, I don't care any more. I've been incredibly blessed with a wife of twenty-four years who loves me in spite of this area of weakness in my life, and we have an incredible relationship, a marriage that I would put up against anyone's. I have four amazing kids who think I'm pretty awesome too, even though they know their dad has some issues. I also have a handful of lifelong friends who think I'm pretty amazing and could care less about my sexual attractions, and of course, God loves me and is not ashamed of me or embarrassed by me; so I don't care any more what anyone else thinks of me. If someone has a problem with the sins I committed almost thirty years ago or with the fact that I live with homosexual attractions, then I figure they're the ones with the problem, not me.

The Most Exciting Part of Your Day

Rick Warren offers some great insight on temptation. The truth about temptation is this: temptation is as much an occasion for you and me do the right thing as it is for us to do the wrong thing.[4] I've realized that experiencing a temptation is a very exciting part of my day! While Satan is using temptation as a weapon of mass destruction in my life, God allows temptation in order for me to develop spiritually. Temptation provides that opportunity of choice for us every day when we get to choose between what is right and what is wrong. Indeed, every time we overcome and defeat the enticement to sin, we become more like Jesus, and that is our ultimate goal in life.

We're all busy. We're all important in some way to someone. Maybe you oversee a huge organization, and hundreds, if not thousands, of men and women and families depend on you for their employment. Perhaps you're a health care provider who literally has the lives of people in your hands. Maybe you're a teacher, and a whole classroom of young and pliable minds is looking to you for wisdom and guidance, or you're a first responder and are one of those brave and rare souls who runs into a situation that everyone else wants to run away from. It could be that you are in the military and are serving your country or are in school getting an education that will allow you to not only enhance your life, but the lives of others through service to your community and fellow man at large. Many reading this are moms and dads with diapers to change and band practice to drive to and little league to coach and meals to make and sick children to comfort and disobedient ones to discipline.

We all have critical roles to play in some form or fashion, and you no doubt will do many essential activities in the next twenty-four-hour period that the world can't do without, but I put before you that there will be very few things you will do that will show your devotion to Jesus more than overcoming the temptations you face. Being confronted with temptation is one of the most significant moments in your day. Temptation is a pivotal instant in time when you, and you alone, have the alternative to do what is right or what is wrong based solely on your own choices.[5] It's one of your big chances to live out your Christianity, your moment in time to decide to be in the light or to stumble in the darkness; you alone, with no church, no minister, no deacon, no elder, no friend, no spouse, but just you, Jesus and the devil watching to see what you will decide. It is one of the few opportunities you will have in this twenty-four-hour period when you can stand and declare to the world, both the physical and the spiritual, whom you have decided to follow.

Temptation is a key instant in time when God and his angels stop to see whether you will just talk about being a follower of Jesus or will actually walk like Jesus. I put before you that there will rarely be a more thrilling part in your day than when you are tempted.

The Necessity of Temptation

In modern-day steelmaking, impurities must be removed from the raw iron, and alloying elements are added to produce the exact steel required. It must be refined and the impurities removed. After it goes through these processes, engineers tell us that the only way the metal can be safely used is after testing it, and it must exceed the testing requirements repeatedly. The metal to be used to make up that Boeing 747 that you're going to get on for your next vacation abroad or business trip must be pure, and in order for it to be purified, it must go through fire. It must be melted and molded to fit the designer's purpose.

The same is true for refining silver. The story is told of a woman who was moved by the idea that God is a refiner and purifier of silver, as portrayed in Malachi 3:3. She wanted to learn more about this process, so she contacted a silversmith and made an appointment to watch him at work.

> As she watched the silversmith, he held a piece of silver over the fire and let it heat up. He explained that in refining silver, one needed to hold the silver in the middle of the fire where the flames were hottest to burn away all the impurities... She asked the silversmith if it was true that he had to sit there in front of the fire the whole time the silver was being heated and refined.
>
> The man answered that he not only had to sit there holding the silver, but he had to keep his eyes on the silver the entire time it was in the fire, until it was completely refined. If the silver was left a moment too long in the flames, it would be destroyed, he said.
>
> The woman was silent for a moment. Then she asked the silversmith, "How do you know when the silver is fully refined?"
>
> He smiled at her and answered, "Oh, that's easy—when I see my image in it."[6]

Just as metal must be molded and purified and, once the impurities are removed, must be tested, we as God's children must be tested before the Lord will be able to use us for his purposes. Just as silver must be purified in fire until the silversmith can see his own reflection, so we are put through the fires (trials and temptations) of life in a manner that if we let it, will allow God to be seen in us. The necessity of trials and temptations teach us several things.

- Satan uses temptation in the hopes that we will sin. God uses temptation to give us freedom of choice and make it possible for us not to sin.

- While temptation is being used as a weapon to make us bad, God uses it to allow us to be good.

- While Satan uses temptation to weaken us, God uses it to make us stronger, finer and purer.

- Temptation is not a penalty; temptation is a privilege because we realize that God is using this as an opportunity to strengthen our spiritual muscles.

The cocoon of the Emperor moth is flasklike in shape. To develop into a perfect insect, it must force its way through the neck of the cocoon by hours of intense struggle. This pressure to which the moth is subjected is nature's way of forcing a life-giving substance into its wings.[7] Sorrow, suffering, trials and tribulations are wisely designed by our creator to grow us into Christlikeness. The refining and developing processes are slow and painful at times, this is true, but they are necessary in order for the impurities to be removed, and through grace, we emerge spiritually alive and ultimately triumphant![8]

In Romans 12:2 Paul calls each of us to "not conform to the pattern of this world, but be transformed by the renewing of your mind. Then you will be able to test and approve what God's will is— his good, pleasing and perfect will."

Our minds are not to be conformed, but transformed. "Conform" means to adhere to; "transform" means to change one's nature. The Greek word for this is where we get the word "metamorphosis."

Metamorphosis is the same word we use to describe what happens to a caterpillar when it changes into a butterfly. What used to inch along the ground in mud and dirt can now soar upward in perfect freedom of flight. That butterfly is the Christian; it is you, it is me, after we have been set free from the mud of sinful behavior, slavery, bondage and the habitual cravings that we used to crawl in daily.[9]

Don't deplore, mourn or regret your temptations and weaknesses; embrace them, celebrate in them, use them as daily opportunities to declare whom you have decided to follow, and allow God to do his work and accomplish his will in the midst of these struggles.

Hope Comes from the Most Unlikely Places

Have you ever heard the story of Jason McElwain? Jason was a seventeen-year-old kid with autism who longed to play basketball but could never make the team. Instead, Jason volunteered to be his high school team's manager in Rochester, New York. He worked hard all year filling water bottles, cleaning the locker room and being the team's number-one fan.

On February 16, 2006, at the final game of the year, however, he was added to the roster by Coach Jim Johnson so he could be given a jersey and get to sit on the bench with the rest of the team. Johnson hoped the situation would even enable him to get McElwain onto the floor for a little playing time. He got the chance with his team up by double digits and four minutes to go. And, in his first action of the year, McElwain missed his first two shots but then sank six three-pointers and another shot, for a total of twenty points in three minutes. "I've had a lot of thrills in coaching," Johnson said. "I've coached a lot of wonderful kids. But I've never experienced such a thrill." The crowd went wild, and his teammates carried the excited McElwain off the court. "I felt like a celebrity!" he beamed. McElwain's mother sees it as a milestone for her son. "This is the first moment Jason has ever succeeded [and could be] proud of himself," reflected Debbie McElwain. "I look at autism as the Berlin Wall, and he cracked it."[10]

Jason is truly one of the least likely basketball heroes ever. He scored twenty points in three minutes. Since that game, millions around the world have since seen this tremendous feat. It was so amazing that George Bush, who was president at the time, said that when he watched it on the news from the residence of the White House, he wept. Three weeks later, the President of the United States met with Jason and his family to congratulate him. Soon after, this seventeen-year-old autistic underdog went on *Oprah, Larry King Live, Good Morning America* and *The Today Show* and was interviewed by every major sports network in North America. McElwain even won the coveted ESPY Award for the Best Moment in Sports in 2006, beating out Kobe Bryant's 81-point game against the Toronto Raptors. But most significant, he has received thousands of letters from all over the world from people whom he has inspired. Many of those letters have come from individuals living with autism who wrote Jason to thank him for giving them hope. Who knew that hope could come in the form of a kid with autism whose job was to fill up water bottles and hand out towels?

You know, in a spiritual sense, we are all Jason McElwains. As Paul says in 1 Corinthians 1:26, "Brothers, think of what you were when you were called. Not many of you were wise by human standards; not many were influential; not many were of noble birth." Every single one of us, before becoming a Christian, had to reach a point in our lives where we realized that we were needy. We had to accept and confess our weaknesses and humbly admit, "I am a sinner, I have made a mess of things, and I can't find my way out."

Look at what God did for us through Jesus: he took us from this foolish, lowly, despised and sinful state and lifted us up to a new reality. We went from being dead in our transgressions and sins to being made alive in Christ (Ephesians 2:1–10).

As Christians, the sky is the limit as to what we can accomplish and the kind of impact we can have on the lives of those around us. We may have our challenges, we will have our physical limitations, we will go through our temptations and have our struggles and our pasts to deal with, but with God on your side, what is it that you cannot accomplish? Do the Scriptures not say, "All things are possible with God?" (Mark 10:27).

Jason didn't realize the impact he was going to have on millions of people when he made those shots. Likewise with us, we often don't see the impact we are having. Often we don't understand how God is using us when we go out onto the court of life.

In Rochester, New York, after that game, Jason went back to being the high school basketball manager until he graduated. But who knew that hope for millions worldwide could come from an unknown seventeen-year-old kid with autism? You, as a Christian, present hope to many: to your family, to those you work with and go to school with, to those in your community and to other Christians in your church family. You have no idea the kind of impact you are having on those around you. You and I give hope by following Christ, by not quitting when things are tough, by doing our best, by learning from our mistakes and by relying on God's forgiveness when we fail.

So thank you for giving an imperfect, sinful man the leeway he needs to give you some pointers on overcoming temptation, the same kind of leeway you would give Michael Jordan, Julia Child, Hank Aaron, Warren Buffett and the apostle Paul. Who knew that hope could come from a guy who lived two decades as a frightened, insecure, frustrated, lonely individual who suffered silently and needlessly for years because he was so terrified that anyone would find out what he struggled with? Who knew that hope would come from...you! But it does. Who knew?

Small Group Discussion Questions

1. Why is it important for us to embrace failure?

2. "What you choose to do with failure is perhaps the most profound indicator of who you are and who you will become" as a Christian. Do you agree or disagree? Why or why not?

3. Do you agree with the assertion that the goal of our lives as Christians is not to stop sinning?

4. Do you agree that it is not a sin to be tempted? Why or why not?

5. How has the idea that being tempted can be the most thrilling part of our day changed your perspective on temptation?

End Notes:_____

1. Christensen, Bert. "Medical Advice to Live By." Bert Christensen's Truth & Humour Collection. 06 July 2015. http://bertc.com/subfour/truth/medicaladvice.htm.

2. Keller, Dr. Timothy. "Sin and Temptation." Sermon, 29 Oct. 1995. Redeemer Presbyterian Church, New York City.

3. Ibid.

4. Warren, Rick. "Growing Through Temptation." *Daily Inspiration for the Purpose Driven Life*. Grand Rapids: Zondervan, 2003.

5. Ibid.

6. Maurus, J. "Forgiving Heart Fosters Peace." *Power of the Heart*. Mumbai: St. Paul, 2008. 102–03.

7. Cook, David. *David C. Cook Lesson Commentary*. Colorado Springs: David C. Cook, 2008. 214.

8. Cowman, L.B. "January 9." *Streams in the Desert*. Grand Rapids: Zondervan, 1996.

9. Ibid.

10. Dakss, Brian. "Autistic Teen's Hoop Dreams Come True." CBS News. 10 Oct. 2008. http://www.cbsnews.com/stories/2006/02/23/earlyshow/main1339324.shtml.

Chapter Two

Kissing God

I never knew how to worship until I knew how
to love.   —Henry Ward Beecher

I prefer not to kiss when others are watching. I'm English Canadian. You may not know this about my countrymen, but we're mostly a shy lot, not the way some other cultures are. Sure, we might give the occasional quick peck to greet each other or to say farewell, congratulate or console, but even those instances are offered only to those closest to us and are not done in public easily; we English Canadians desire to keep our lips to ourselves when we're out and about. French Canadians, well, that's something else. The French are more unabashed than their English counterparts and will kiss you twice, once on each cheek for both your coming and going. The Belgians will kiss you three times. In Mediterranean and Latin countries, men traditionally kiss each other; again, not so much in Canada.

Regardless of your local custom or frequency when it comes to puckering up, though, no matter what culture you come from, kissing is a part of the human experience. We kiss lovers on the lips, infants on the head and children on their cuts and bruises. In fact, kissing plays many roles in human affairs, and our folklore, rituals and everyday behavior are full of examples. Gamblers kiss their cards, patriots kiss their native soul, politicians kiss babies and princesses kiss frogs to turn them into princes.

At a Minnesota renaissance festival, on September 12, 1998, Alfred Wolfram from New Brighton, Minnesota kissed 11,030 people in eight hours—over twenty-two people a minute. I've seen pictures of Mr. Wolfram; not that much of a looker, if I may say so, which leaves me wondering why on earth over eleven thousand people would stand in line for hours on end to have Alfred's sloppy wet lips press up against theirs! Imagine being the poor sucker (pun intended) who was number 11,030? I suppose the other attractions at this festival left a lot to be desired.

There's even a world record for the longest kiss! Of course, world records change all the time, but as of the writing of this book, the current Guinness world record for nonstop smooching was accomplished in 2013 and lasted fifty-eight hours, thirty-five minutes and fifty-eight seconds, achieved by two people from Thailand with very tired and numb lips.

Kissing has been around for as long as we have, it seems. The ancient Romans were the kissingest culture that ever existed. They puckered up on every conceivable occasion, and it became popular to perfume one's mouth with oriental spices to enhance the pleasure of a kiss. In fact, they kissed so much that Emperor Tiberius banned the canoodle from Roman society to stop the spread of disease. The King of England issued a proclamation banning the kiss throughout England in 1439 as a response to the outbreak of the plague.

And then there's the Bible. Kissing is very much a biblical theme. There was Judas' kiss of betrayal, the woman who kissed Jesus' feet and anointed them with oil, the kiss of the prodigal's father, the kiss of the early church, otherwise known as the "holy kiss" (2 Corinthians 13:12), and there's this in John 4:24 (NASB): "God is spirit, and those who worship Him must worship in spirit and truth."

How We Kiss God

So you're probably asking, what does kissing have to do with worshipping God in spirit and in truth? Everything! That's because the Greek word for "worship" in this passage literally means "to kiss." There are three Greek terms that are rendered by the English word "worship": *latreuo* which means "to give service" (used four times), *sebazomai*, which means "to idolize" (used once) and *prosuneo*, which means "to kiss" (used fifty-eight times). This last is the term most frequently used, by far, to describe the kind of worship we are to offer God; it means "to kiss God." So, "God is spirit, and those who worship him must worship in spirit and truth" literally says that God is spirit and those who *kiss him* must *kiss him* in spirit and truth. In Acts 8:27 the Ethiopian Eunuch had gone to Jerusalem to worship or to "kiss." In Acts 24:11 Paul tells the Roman Governor Felix that he had gone just twelve days earlier to Jerusalem to worship or "kiss." The literal translation of this word for "kiss" is "to adore" or to have the "highest respect for."[1]

Our first-century brothers and sisters, those whose lives make up the book of Acts, had an understanding of what worship to God meant that I think often eludes us today. I don't know about you, but if I'm going to kiss someone that I adore or have the highest respect for, I want to have a relationship with him or her first. In fact, I only want to kiss those I'm closest to. I don't just adore everyone. It is only those whom I am most intimate that I would even consider kissing.

When Jesus said these words as recorded in John 4, they were considered radical, mind-blowing, controversial, unheard of! Palestine had become a drowsy place; God had become an entity and worship a thing to do. But Jesus, by his teaching, shook religion out of its sleep. Everywhere he went, men and women were stirred by what they saw and heard and cried out in astonishment, "No one ever spoke the way this man does!" (see John 7:46). Jesus was crying out to a people caught up in stuffy religion with no heart and all ceremony to fall in love with God with the kind of love that would envelope every nook and cranny of their souls. Likewise, today, John 4 cries out to you and me to not merely go to church or read our Bibles or sing some songs or say some legalistic prayers, but to be so personal, so intimate, so delicate, so special, so near, so dear, so full of respect in this relationship with God that our bond is like that of two people who love each other so deeply that they would be moved to share one of the most personal expressions of love that one can demonstrate to another human being: a kiss.

This is the kind of relationship that the Lord longs to have with each of us; following God is not about rules and obligations; it's about relationship. The primary purpose of the Bible is to tell a love story about a Father (God) wanting to lavish his affection on his children (you and me); the Scriptures firmly establish this from Genesis to Revelation. The scriptures below speak of intimacy, familiarity, friendship, kindness, mercy, protection and confidence in this two-way relationship.

> Yet you, LORD, are our Father.
>> We are the clay, you are the potter;
>> we are all the work of your hand. (Isaiah 64:8)

> The LORD disciplines those he loves,
>> as a father the son he delights in. (Proverbs 3:12)

> As a father has compassion on his children,
>> so the LORD has compassion on those who fear him;
> for he knows how we are formed,
>> he remembers that we are dust. (Psalm 103:13–14)

> "Look at the birds of the air; they do not sow or reap or store away in barns, and yet your heavenly Father feeds them. Are you not much more valuable than they?" (Matthew 6:26)

> "Do not be afraid, little flock, for your Father has been pleased to give you the kingdom." (Luke 12:32)

> "Do not let your hearts be troubled. Trust in God; trust also in me. In my Father's house are many rooms; if it were not so, I would have told you. I am going there to prepare a place for you." (John 14:1–2 NIV1984)

> "No, the Father himself loves you because you have loved me and have believed that I came from God." (John 16:27)

> For you did not receive a spirit that makes you a slave again to fear, but you received the Spirit of sonship. And by him we cry, "Abba, Father." The Spirit himself testifies with our spirit that we are God's children. (Romans 8:15–16 NIV1984)

> "Which of you, if his son asks for bread, will give him a
> stone? Or if he asks for a fish, will give him a snake? If you, then,
> though you are evil, know how to give good gifts to your children,
> how much more will your Father in heaven give good gifts to
> those who ask him!" (Matthew 7:9–11)

> How great is the love the Father has lavished on us, that we
> should be called children of God! And that is what we are!
> (1 John 3:1 NIV1984)

Understanding the Father-child relationship that the Scriptures clearly describe is essential to your long-term success as a faithful follower of Christ. If your view of God is that of only a spiritual entity that is to be feared or held in awe, you'll be missing one of the most beautiful and heartwarming aspects of what God intended for us to enjoy when he created us. We are to fear and be in awe, clearly. But pity the follower of God who hasn't been able to couple the omnipotent and omnipresent qualities that drive us to our knees in humble praise, with the quality that God is a loving Dad who is intimately concerned about every detail of our lives, cares for us, is gentle with us and is eager for a two-way relationship.

Who's Your Daddy?

I grew up on Dufferin Street in Windsor, Ontario, Canada, just across the American border from Detroit, Michigan. In the mid-1970s, Windsor was a grimy industrial city filled with Chrysler auto factories that mass-produced tens of thousands of Dodge Darts, Chrysler Cobras and Dodge Chargers for the North American auto market. My best friend was David Norris. In the winter we played street hockey out in the frigid cold in front of my house until long after dark, and at the end of every day, I always won the Stanley Cup. In the summer it was baseball, and I was also always the hero of the game! (I know; I had problems as a kid; my therapist is helping me deal with my fantasy-prone personality.)

One hot summer afternoon when I was thirteen or fourteen years old, Davey and I were at our usual place, playing catch. To the average onlooker, it was two urchins throwing a baseball around, but in my mind's eye, I was Rusty Staub, the famous Detroit Tigers six-time all-star centerfielder, and we were in game seven of the World Series, ahead by one run in the bottom of the ninth, with two outs and a man on second. As the fans went wild and I yelled out the play-by-play like they do on television, no doubt driving the neighbors crazy, the imaginary batter hit a double. In my attempt to imitate Rusty hurling the ball to home plate to get out the runner rounding third, the ball wildly flew far to the right and instead of landing in Davey's glove and thereby allowing us to be catapulted into baseball immortality, it smashed through the window of a house belonging to an elderly lady who lived across the street. Sorry, Rusty, I let you down! The sound of breaking glass filled the air, and we two dopey kids looked at each other with terror in our eyes. "Best friend" David suddenly bolted down the street, no longer interested in World Series glory.

I was left standing there abandoned, knowing my baseball career was over forever. Where could I go? The only place I knew to go was home, to my dad. I knew he'd be mad, but he would help me. (I certainly couldn't go to mom; she'd kill me; mom was the disciplinarian of the family, and she did her job well!) Of course with dad, I received the lecture that every father gives their kid when they break a window, even during game seven of the World Series, then he rightly grabbed me by the collar and marched me over to the poor old lady's place to apologize, and then made me cough up for the new window out of my allowance until it was paid off, which seemed to take until I was old enough to drive. I was in trouble that day, no doubt, but dad was there and he helped me through it, albeit somewhat angrily when I first confessed; but by the end of the ordeal he was patting me on the back, telling me it was going to be OK and all was forgiven. Then we both agreed that what mother doesn't know won't hurt her, or us!

Isn't that how it's supposed to be? When you're in trouble and you need help, go to Dad. I mean, where else should you go when life hits you hard? To a stranger? No, you go where there is safety and support and protection and love. I realize that for many reading this, these words are not representative of the kind of relationship you had with your earthly father, but it is the ideal. I, as a sinful and imperfect creature, possess these qualities quite insufficiently, regardless of my best attempts. (I'm doing my best to be good to my kids; after all, they'll pick my nursing home!) However, God as the perfect Father possesses these characteristics completely and perfectly, which is why when trouble comes, there is no better place to go than to Dad, my heavenly Father.

Tempt-Away Step 1: Pray Immediately

Yeah, I know; it's obvious. Step 1 of the Tempt-Away plan to overcome every temptation you face in sixty seconds or less is to pray immediately. But ask yourself, if it's so obvious, why do we so often skip it? And notice that Step 1 is not to just pray, but to pray *immediately*; and by that I mean the second you notice that you are undergoing a temptation. In fact, there should be as little space as possible between the time you first recognize the urge to sin and when you are quickly offering up a few words to your Father for help and assistance. I'm not talking about you praying a doxology that would move the masses to tears or leave theologians with enough material to author commentaries around it, just a brief prayer, say fifteen seconds or so, asking God for help in your time of need. "Lord, I need your help. Right now I am tempted to sin. I do not want to fail you so I am giving this situation to you. Help me stay strong and glorify you with my life. Thank you for believing in me when I'm not sure I believe in myself. Amen."

That's a good prayer, right there! I've said it many, many times. Or, it can be as quick and as simple as "God, help me. I'm in trouble; I can't get through this alone!"

Suzanne Woods Fisher once said, "Opportunity may knock once, but temptation bangs on your front door forever." We need to realize that we're no match for the testing we face unless we face it with the power of the Holy Spirit. The quickest way for you to fail a test of your faith is to think you've got the power to pass it on your own. If you want to fail when tested with temptation, then face the seduction by yourself, on your own power, with your own authority.

Is it possible to overcome temptation without prayer? Of course, I've done that often, as well. But it's not a good long-term strategy and does not guarantee success. It also leaves one missing out on all of the benefits that come from turning to God in prayer. If it's your custom to defeat temptation without immediate prayer, you might indeed overcome temptation occasionally, but is that the only goal we should have in this spiritual battle, not to sin? As I stated in the previous chapter, the goal of our lives as Christians *should not* be to stop sinning, but to love God and strive to glorify him with our lives. Defeating the temptation to sin is just one ingredient of many that combine to create a close, intimate relationship with our Father. So, if it's your norm to try to defeat the enticement to sin on your own fuel, you are robbing yourself of the incredible and beautiful opportunity to give your Dad a kiss, and robbing your heavenly Dad of his opportunity to be intimate with you, to fight for you, and to be in solidarity with you in your moment of weakness.

Besides these realities, to face temptations with immediate prayer breaks us free from the prideful and arrogant posture that the world celebrates but that God hates, and one that seemingly comes so naturally to most of us: that of prideful independence.

Most in the world today will say that the way to honor is through self-strength and self-reliance. God tells us the way to true honor is to be a man or woman of great humility, both before God and before others. 1 Peter 5:6 says, "Humble yourselves, therefore, under God's mighty hand, that he may lift you up in due time."

Lord, It's Hard to Be Humble!

It's not easy initiating an authentic account of what challenges we are suffering, is it? Not even with God! One reason is because sometimes the temptations, thoughts and longings that cross our minds are so evil, not to mention occasionally even illegal, that it's hard to admit the depth of the wickedness even to ourselves, much less anyone else. Have you ever been tempted to get out of your car and beat the guy in front of you senseless with a crowbar for driving like a maniac, or at least quickly fantasize about it, or am I the only one? We know that Romans 3:10 is absolutely correct when it says that "there is no one righteous, not even one." We're all broken and we've all had thoughts, desires, fantasies, attractions and tantalizations enter or rise to our conscious minds that are so out of bounds, so completely out of character and so far from how we desire to live in Christ that it's difficult to admit, even to ourselves, that we would be capable of such a thing, much less confess it to someone else, including God. Come on; let's be real here. I can't be the only sinful wretch out there!

Fake Kisses

Another reason why authenticity with God is so difficult is a little more obvious: we simply want to look good, both to ourselves and to God, as if we could somehow impress him! Having to admit to even the Lord that we are sometimes this wicked is not easy. It's funny how we can try to pass ourselves off in front of one who is omnipresent, who knows every thought in our mind and every word spoken and every intention of our heart. It's not like he is surprised by what we are capable of; he knows it already; that's why he sent Jesus to save us! Wait a minute, Guy. I thought this chapter was supposed to be about prayer. Well, it is. You see, many Christians are so intent on looking good and hiding their weaknesses that not only are they afraid to boast about them with the people in their lives, they don't want to acknowledge them before God either, as if they could somehow fool even the Lord into thinking that they are good and have nothing to confess. If the first step to defeating temptation is to turn to God in immediate, brief prayer, we've got to first be prepared and even enthusiastic to tell God just how wicked our thoughts and desires sometimes are. Be honest with yourself, be honest with people you trust, and be honest especially with God. This is what intimacy is all about. God can tell when our kisses are fake.

When Judas betrayed the Lord with a kiss, Matthew (26:47–50) and Mark (14:43–45) use the Greek verb *kataphilein* which means to kiss tenderly or passionately. Ouch! It's amazing how passionate our prayers can seem, how deep and powerful and meaningful they may sound, yet all the while, our hearts can be so far away that we are not honest in our communication, and all we're really doing is throwing fake kisses at the Lord. We may be able to fool everyone else, but if we are to have real power to overcome temptation, gut-level honesty with the Lord the moment temptation enters our consciousness is required. There's no need to be embarrassed about what kind of sinful desires you're facing or what attractions you have. We're all broken, we're all a mess, and it's messy for everyone. Again, this does not surprise God and is why he sent Jesus. I'll use Hebrews 4:14–16 again, as it only confirms this:

> *Therefore, since we have a great high priest who has ascended into heaven, Jesus the Son of God, let us hold firmly*

to the faith we profess. For we do not have a high priest who is unable to sympathize with our weaknesses, but we have one who has been tempted in every way, just as we are—yet he did not sin. Let us then approach God's throne of grace with confidence, so that we may receive mercy and find grace to help us in our time of need.

No Need to Be Alone

Going to God in prayer immediately at the point of temptation also causes us to become dependent on our spiritual Father for his power because we're not facing it alone. Who wants to go through difficulty, challenges and spiritual battles solo, and why would you do so when it's not necessary? Often, when Satan whispers his lure we will physically be alone, or at least not have any other Christians in the immediate vicinity from whom to find encouragement. Whether you are sitting in a classroom struggling to stay awake, at work, on a bus, walking down a busy street, 35,000 feet in the air watching a movie on that little screen on the seat in front of you, standing on the crowded subway, driving to a business meeting, at home changing the umpteenth diaper, wherever; you will regularly not have anyone nearby who you can count on to offer support. However, with the blessing of prayer, you will have at your disposal the creator of the universe and all of the benefits that come with that relationship.

Don't Touch the Queen!

On April 1, 2009, an event took place in London, England that shook the world and almost destroyed forever the international relations between Great Britain and the United States: Michelle Obama touched the queen! That's right, the horrifying and stunning event took place in Buckingham Palace at the start of a G-20 summit during a reception that Her Majesty was hosting for world leaders.

There is quite a protocol that must be followed when meeting the Queen of England, and these strict rules are in place for everyone, including presidents and first ladies. At the top of the list is the no-touch rule. If one comes face to face with the British monarch, one must wait until she extends her hand, and only then may they take it, but only gently, and upon taking her hand into theirs, one must not pump her hand up and down as in a handshake, but rather hold it limply for only the quickest moment while they either slightly curtsy or bow. Of course, there can be absolutely no hugging, no kissing of the cheek, no touching of the shoulder or putting one's arm around the sovereign's midsection or God forbid, any kind pat or slap of the royal backside!

Yet in spite of these protocols, here was Mrs. Obama actually putting her arm around the royal shoulders and keeping it there while the two of them chatted, like two close friends. The British press was aghast! It made headlines literally all over the world. Over and over again the horrifying episode was replayed on national newscasts. Most could never tell you what the prime ministers and presidents decided in relation to international politics at that G-20 summit, but everyone knew that the First Lady of the United States had put her arm around the Queen. It was a devastating moment for all, no doubt!

Being able to meet the Queen or King of England is no easy feat to accomplish. Unless you are being knighted or are the leader of a country, the chances of being able to do so are almost impossible. About the only opportunity a "normal" person would ever have of greeting the royal monarch in person would be to stand at the edge of a rope line as she does a "walkabout" to meet the everyday folk, as she sometimes does when she travels, and even then if you were fortunate enough to actually speak with her, you would only be able to get a few words out before she moved on.

I even speak from personal experience. In June 2010 Her Majesty came to the city that my family and I were living in at the time, Halifax, Nova Scotia. Being a good English Canadian, and not ever having had the opportunity to see Canada's queen in person, I was determined to go and lugged my family along with me (my four kids were thrilled—NOT!). To make matters really difficult, it rained buckets that day and we were all drenched. To get a spot to see her, we arrived hours before she did, but even in the rain the crowds were heavy and it was not possible to get near the area where she would do her walkabout. There was a marked-off section where she would stop to briefly speak to onlookers, but for this event, these fortunate few were chosen beforehand and only those who had special tickets were allowed to enter this designated area. Not being "special," we had to watch from quite a distance, so far away, in fact, that we saw more of her on a large-screen monitor that had been set up than we did of her in person. Having been raised in a family that believed in the importance of the monarchy (Scottish heritage), I appreciated being there, although my four kids didn't cherish the opportunity, especially since it rained hard enough for us to row home when the event was over.

Regardless of how you feel about the role the queen has, whether you are a fan or not, you can't argue the global impact the position holds. Elizabeth the Second, as leader of the Commonwealth, is queen over fifty-three countries that span all six continents and include 2.1 billion people, almost a third of the entire world's population. That's serious clout.

The queen's official title is much more than what you would at first think. It's not just "Elizabeth the Second, Queen of England." No, her actual title is...are you ready? This is no joke:

Her Majesty Elizabeth the Second, by the Grace of God, of Great Britain, Ireland and the British Dominions beyond the Seas, Defender of the Faith, Duchess of Edinburgh, Countess of Merioneth, Baroness Greenwich, Duke of Lancaster, Lord of Mann, Duke of Normandy, Sovereign of the Most Honourable Order of the Garter, Sovereign of the Most Honourable Order of the Bath, Sovereign of the Most Ancient and Most Noble Order of the Thistle, Sovereign of the Most Illustrious Order of Saint Patrick, Sovereign of the Most Distinguished Order of Saint Michael and Saint George, Sovereign of the Most Excellent Order of the British Empire, Sovereign of the Distinguished Service Order, Sovereign of the Imperial Service Order, Sovereign of the Most Exalted Order of the Star of India, Sovereign of the Most Eminent Order of the Indian Empire, Sovereign of the Order of British India, Sovereign of the Indian Order of Merit, Sovereign of the Order of Burma, Sovereign of the Royal Order of Victoria and Albert, Sovereign of the Royal Family Order of King Edward VII, Sovereign of the Order of Merit, Sovereign of the Order of the Companions of Honour, Sovereign of the Royal Victorian Order, Sovereign of the Most Venerable Order of the Hospital of St John of Jerusalem.

Imagine putting that on your business card! Why are we discussing the Queen of England? Because she is the most famous woman on earth, certainly one of the wealthiest, and one of the most influential human beings on the planet. When she dies, her son Prince Charles will be king, and when he's gone, Prince William will be; and they will be equal to her in wealth and influence, no doubt. But what are these people compared to God, your spiritual father? Indeed, if we were to take all of the queens and kings and prime ministers and presidents who have ever lived and combine all of their money and power and wealth, who would they be compared to God?

May all kings bow down to him
and all nations serve him. (Psalm 72:11)

He brings princes to naught
and reduces the rulers of this world to nothing.
No sooner are they planted,
no sooner are they sown,
no sooner do they take root in the ground,
than he blows on them and they wither,
and a whirlwind sweeps them away like chaff.
(Isaiah 40:23–24)

Therefore God exalted him to the highest place
and gave him the name that is above every name,
that at the name of Jesus every knee should bow,
in heaven and on earth and under the earth,
and every tongue acknowledge that Jesus Christ is Lord,
to the glory of God the Father. (Philippians 2:9–11)

The heavens receded like a scroll being rolled up, and every mountain and island was removed from its place.
Then the kings of the earth, the princes, the generals, the rich, the mighty, and everyone else, both slave and free, hid in caves and among the rocks of the mountains. They called to the mountains and the rocks, "Fall on us and hide us from the face of him who sits on the throne and from the wrath of the Lamb! For the great day of their wrath has come, and who can withstand it?" (Revelation 6:14–17)

In light of these passages, Queen Elizabeth doesn't look that impressive anymore, even with that ridiculously long title, does she? Nor does anyone else, for that matter. Every ruler in the history of the world: Adolf Hitler, Joseph Stalin, Abraham Lincoln, Mahatma Gandhi, Winston Churchill, Saddam Hussein, Ronald Reagan, Emperor Hirohito, Bill Clinton, Mikhail Gorbachev, Barak Obama, Vladimir Putin, Margaret Thatcher, Augustus Caesar, Nelson Mandela, John F. Kennedy, Napoleon Bonaparte, Alexander the Great, Sir John A. MacDonald (sorry, I had to throw a Canadian in there), whomever you choose; they will all one day bow on bended knee, confess that Jesus is Lord, and worship the King of Kings. He is Lord of heaven, Lord of earth, he is Lord of all who reigns, he is Lord of the entire universe, and he is God, your heavenly Father. Every celebrity that modern culture has ever idolized and worshipped, including Michael Jackson, Robert DeNiro, Elvis, Tom Cruise, John Lennon, Marilyn Monroe, Bono, Jay Z, Michelle Pfeiffer, Oprah, Leonardo DiCaprio, or any of the "stars" who are yet to be discovered, will bend their knee to him. You get the point, right? They are all brilliant entertainers and performers and we've all been recipients of their extreme talent, but even for the wealthiest and most famous and glamorous among us, the time will come (prayerfully in this life if they are still breathing) when they will each bow down, as we all must, worship God and proclaim that "Jesus is Lord!"

In spite of all this, to get to speak to God, the creator of the universe, there are no rope lines, no security checks to go through and no Secret Service to get past. You don't need to make an appointment or be an important person to get to talk to him. No ticket necessary. He does not care about how much money you do or do not have. He is not interested in title or position. He is not impressed with what you own or what kind of education you have or have not received. He is always available, twenty-four hours a day, every day, and he is always eager to hear from you, no matter in what circumstance you find yourself. His love has no limits, his forgiveness is unending and he is the one reaching out to you, hoping you will respond, because he is more than your God, he is your Father. That is to whom I am suggesting we turn in prayer when we first notice temptation in our lives.

Our Lifeline

In humans, during the nine months of pregnancy, while an infant is growing and developing, he or she is connected to the outside world in the uterus of the mother by an amazing handiwork of God's creation. This connection is called the umbilical cord. This amazing little gadget brings nutrients from the mother into the fetus, so that the infant will grow and develop. It also brings to the little tyke a fresh supply of oxygenated blood so that it can circulate through the child's circulatory system. Then, when the blood has circulated through the fetus, this umbilical cord carries the blood from the child back to the mother, to be sent through her system, into the heart, lungs and other vital organs to be rejuvenated and to have oxygen added. Then it passes back to the unborn in a continuous circular motion. Not only that, but the umbilical cord also carries waste from the fetus into the mother's disposal system, where it is eliminated along with her own waste.

If the cord becomes kinked, knotted or severed, or otherwise disconnected, the unborn fetus is in trouble—*big* trouble, because its only line of survival has been interrupted. In a short time the fetus will die and there will be no way to revive it.

Prayer is our spiritual umbilical cord to God. Through this exercise, God sends us his love, gives us peace and gives us life. Through it we are given the spiritual strength and nutrients that we need to survive, and through it as well, we can get rid of the waste in our lives. The problem is, most of humanity has allowed this spiritual umbilical cord to become kinked, knotted, severed or disconnected, or even discarded entirely.

I've often considered Paul's admonition in 1 Thessalonians 5:16–18 to be, well, forgive me, but...unrealistic. "Rejoice *always*, pray *continually*, give thanks in all circumstances; for this is God's will for you in Christ Jesus" (emphasis mine). Don't get me wrong; it would be great if I could actually do all three of those as completely as he says, but I confess, I fall way short. The words "always," "continually" and "all," are just so complete and all-encompassing.

However, when I actually live out what I'm prescribing in this book—when the very first thing I do is pray the moment temptation enters my mind—it actually makes it much more realistic that I can indeed "pray continually" than if I put my prayer life in a box saying,

"From this time to that time, I will pray."

Consider King David and his prayer life as recorded for us in the Psalms. Truly, praying was a morning, afternoon, evening and nighttime affair for him.

- **Psalm 5:1–3**—in the morning
- **Psalm 42:8**—in the daytime and in the night
- **Psalm 55:16–18**—in the evening, in the morning and at noon
- **Psalm 63:1, 6–8**—early in the morning and late at night while he was in bed
- **Psalm 108:1–4**—at dawn
- **Psalm 113:3**—from the rising of the sun to its going down
- **Psalm 149:5–6**—at night while in bed

Prayer with his Lord was surely more than something that was relegated to only a set time. Prayer was something continuous because he so clearly saw his desperate need for it in his life. If you really do pray immediately when you feel temptation creeping in on you, you will discover a new prayer life and reliance on the Lord that will assist with your ability to "pray continually." The spiritual umbilical cord called prayer will be fulfilling its purpose of providing you the spiritual nutrients you need for survival while eliminating the waste, all in a continual, circular motion.

If It's Good Enough for Jesus...

In our attempt to imitate the life of Christ and how he handled the difficulties, challenges and temptations that he faced daily, we need to imitate the reliance he had on his Father for sustenance, courage and strength. If it was good enough for him...

Possibly no better testimony about the kind of life that Jesus lived can be found than the one given by those who had him killed. While Jesus was hanging from that piece of wood on Golgotha, gasping for breath, those who stood watching laughed and said spiteful things. Among this group of gawkers were most likely members of the Sanhedrin, the chief priests, the scribes and the leaders. They all joined in gruesome unison and ridiculed and scorned him. It is incredible how human beings could be so diabolical as to sneer and laugh at a man in the hour of his death. Amazingly, when they put their collective insults together, the climax of their assault was this, as recorded Matthew 27:43: "He trusts in God. Let God rescue him now if he wants him, for he said, 'I am the Son of God.'"

There is much to learn here about the prayer life of Christ. When the worst accusation his murderers could charge him of was relying on God, that's pretty incredible. May my enemies attack me with as much when my time comes! Jesus' whole life was proof that he trusted in God, from the time when as a boy he said to his mother, "Didn't you know I had to be in my Father's house?" (Luke 2:49) to his dying words on the cross, "Father, into your hands I commit my spirit" (Luke 23:46). From the beginning of his life to the end, he trusted in his Father, and that trust was never broken.

Many a person has for years trusted in God, only to discover that when times were really bad their trust in God was not strong enough to get them through. Sin gets us down. Disappointment may do it. Our dreams don't come true, and failure in life can hit us hard. One disappointment after another may come until we feel hopeless and wonder, "Where is God?" When we stop trusting and turning to the one we love, the one we've been kissing, we become suspicious, we doubt their abilities, and their love becomes suspect. When this happens with God, our relationship with him becomes cold, hard, rigid and impersonal; it goes from a relationship to a religion.

Jesus had all of the dark experiences possible for a person to have; yet he did not let his lifeline to his Father be disconnected. He was maligned and abused and denounced and left all alone. He was accused of blasphemy and treason and of being Satan himself, yet his heart remained true to his Father. He kept crying out, "Not my will, but yours be done" (Luke 22:42).

Exodus 34:14 tells us that God is a "jealous" God. When temptation comes calling, where will you turn? Who will you worship? Who will you kiss? Let God have the situations you face and the fear you have about failing him. Leave the temptation at his feet and thank God for his power, love and belief in you.

That is Step 1 of the Tempt-Away plan to overcome every temptation you face in sixty seconds or less—a quick prayer.

Step 1: Pray. 15 seconds

Often that is enough to end the enticement to sin, and the other three steps will not be necessary, but if after that prayer Satan is still whispering, you need to move quickly to Step 2.

Small Group Discussion Questions

1. If the term "worship" means "to kiss," how will that change the way you view worship in the future?

2. Why do we have such a difficult time accepting God's love and his desire to have an intimate relationship with us and so quickly go towards following rules and obligations and being religious?

3. In what ways can we be like Judas, covering Jesus tenderly with fake kisses?

4. Jesus prayed when faced with temptation. Why do we so often avoid praying when we are being tempted?

5. How is prayer like a spiritual umbilical cord?

End Note:_____

1. "Worship (Verb and Noun), Worshiping." https://www.blueletterbible.org/search/Dictionary/viewTopic.cfm?topic=VT0003400 Strong's Number: g4352.

Chapter Three

Live Your Life On Purpose

Efforts and courage are not enough without purpose and direction. —John F. Kennedy

I'm not a presidential historian; I'm not even American, so I'm sure there are those who could speak with more authority on this issue, but may I say that to me, an admitted novice when it comes to American political history, that Theodore Roosevelt, the twenty-sixth president of the United States, does not seem to have been your typical politician. The guy was much more than an officeholder; the two-term president was an author, boxing champion, war hero, authentic cowboy, local sheriff, avid outdoorsman and conservationist, too. As an interesting side note, in 1902 the Governor of Mississippi took the president on a hunting trip. Near the end of the day, most on the excursion had already killed an animal, except Theodore Roosevelt. Wanting to help the president be successful, some assistants had cornered a small black bear, even going so far as to club it half unconscious and then tie it to a tree, inviting Mr. Roosevelt to shoot the trapped animal. The President was horrified and refused, claiming that it was unsportsmanlike.

When newspapers wrote about the incident the next day, this President of the United States was nicknamed "Teddy Bear." A New York City candy-store owner by the name of Morris Michtom read the story and had his wife sew the very first children's stuffed bear, hoping it would sell in their candy store. They called it the Teddy Bear. Soon poor old Mrs. Michtom couldn't keep up with the demand as she sewed like a madwoman in the basement of that store, so they had the stuffed animal mass-produced and millions of moms and dads from around the world rushed out to purchase one. Eventually Mr. and Mrs. Michtom left the candy-store business forever and started their own toy company: the Ideal Toy Company, which became one of the largest toymakers in the world and remained so for almost eighty years. The company's last big success was the Rubik's Cube in the mid-1980s before the Ideal Toy Company finally closed up shop. And that's the rest of the story!

Wow; sorry, I just went way off track there! This chapter has absolutely nothing to do with the history of the teddy bear or toymaking. Back to the real Theodore Roosevelt: I'm not an American...he was not your average politician...author, cowboy, boxing champion, soldier...oh yeah, right, I remember now: he was also quite a wordsmith. If you ever need some inspiration, Google the quotes of Theodore Roosevelt: "Believe you can, and you're halfway there." "Keep your eyes on the stars and your feet on the ground." "Nobody cares how much you know, until they know how much you care." "The only man who never makes a mistake is the man who never does anything." And then there's my favorite: "A thorough knowledge of the Bible is worth more than a college education." Pretty cool, right? Here's my second favorite Theodore Roosevelt quote: "In any moment of decision, the best thing you can do is the right thing, the next best thing is the wrong thing, and the worst thing you can do is nothing!" Sage advice. Those words have helped me many, many times over the years.

Tempt-Away Step 2: Get Moving!

And this leads us to Step 2 of the Tempt-Away plan on how to defeat every temptation you face in less than sixty seconds. Step 1 is to pray immediately; just a few brief words to your heavenly Father telling him you need help, a quick kiss. That will often be enough to end the temptation and have Satan fleeing. But if after that prayer the temptation is still banging at your front door, then escalate your energies to Step 2, which is to GET MOVING! You must be purposeful. Go! I mean physically. Don't just sit there! As Teddy Bear said, "The worst thing you can do is nothing!" MOVE IT! NOW! QUICKLY! WITH NO TIME TO WASTE! Do it deliberately. Live your life on purpose. Don't let life happen to you; take life by the horns and take charge. You're not a victim, so don't live like one. Get up and move! The quick fifteen-second prayer was the best place to start, but now it's time to get going.

Turn the channel, turn off the television, get off the couch, turn down another street, get out of that neighborhood, shut your mouth and get away before one more vile word spews out of you, delete that app, turn off that computer, put the phone down, get out of the bed, cross the street, shut down that iPad, get off the bus, put the burger down, put your credit card back in your wallet and leave the mall, finish that conversation and get away before you start gossiping and slandering, put your hands in your pockets and get out of that store before you take something that is not yours, escape from those "friends" who are pressuring you, stop talking and leave the room before you have that toothpaste-out-of-the-tube moment with your spouse or child. You have to actually, physically move your body on purpose. GET MOVING!

Movement Science

This is more than just a cute little corrective step in overcoming temptation, and it is more than us physically removing ourselves from the source of the temptation, although that is also a smart thing to do, as we will discuss next. There is emerging scientific proof that physical movement changes our brain. I'm not talking about only rigorous exercise such as running five miles, although certainly if you were to do that when facing a temptation, I'm sure you would have forgotten what caused you to start running to begin with, by the time you crawled back into your house half unconscious. I'm saying that even low-intensity activity, even the simplest action, can help shift your brain to focusing on something other than the initial temptation you are facing. Many support groups and 12 step programs advocate the "move a muscle, change a thought" philosophy. Of course, the brain is incredibly complex and has been called the final frontier of science.

A hundred billion neurons, close to a quadrillion connections between them, and we don't even fully understand a single cell. Neuroscience [is] where psychology meets biology. And with new tools at our disposal—computer simulations, medical imaging—we double our knowledge every decade.[1]

Quoting Steve Sisgold, a body-movement therapist and expert in this field, *Psychology Today* reports on his experience in assisting his patients and says:

A client will be stuck in some unproductive thought loop or knee-jerk reaction. They become fuzzy and confused as to what is actually occurring right in front of them. I redirect their attention to the movements happening in their body, which consistently opens a window to solutions that aren't being arrived at by the mind alone. Clients find the attention-shift consistently generates new insight [and] enhances creative thinking and resiliency. They just seem smarter once they are conscious of how their body moves. We have the ability and hardwiring to use movement awareness to discover and break the neural nets that work against us.

He continues to prove his point with this exercise:

Open your arms wide, or raise your hand in a high-five, or mimic Steve Martin doing his "wild and crazy guy" shoulder shimmy. Sync that movement with your breathing and notice how that changes your mood. How did that feel? Do you notice a change in your thinking or energy level? Make that choice to pause and make expansive moves as often as you can. It can make a big difference in how you feel, make decisions or react to a situation.[2]

I don't know about you, but when I'm in the midst of temptation, when I'm weak in my faith, when I'm facing discouragement and struggling through life, and then Satan attempts to take advantage of my spiritually fragile state, I can come very close to what was just described: being stuck in some unproductive thought loop or knee-jerk reaction and being fuzzy and confused as to what is actually occurring. Often when Satan comes calling, our minds (and convictions) are dull and sluggish. Now, I'm not suggesting that when we are tempted with sin, we all start doing the "wild and crazy guy" shoulder shimmy, although that would be pretty entertaining to watch (not getting the "wild and crazy guy" reference? Welcome to the 1970s. It was a Steve Martin shtick on *Saturday Night Live*). However, there is no doubt that body movement affects our thinking; physical movement can awaken a dull mind and help us focus on something else. When temptation comes upon us, it first enters our thought world, and the Bible is full of scriptures that challenge us to deal with temptations at that level. Here are just two examples, but I could have provided many more:

> *Do not conform to the pattern of this world, but be transformed by the renewing of your mind. Then you will be able to test and approve what God's will is—his good, pleasing and perfect will.* (Romans 12:2)

> *You were taught, with regard to your former way of life, to put off your old self, which is being corrupted by its deceitful desires; to be made new in the attitude of your minds; and to put on the new self, created to be like God in true righteousness and holiness.* (Ephesians 4:22–24)

So if the problem starts in our minds, that is where the battle must be fought, and one of the keys to doing this successfully is to move our bodies. You will be amazed at how often the temptation you are facing will suddenly decrease or even disappear completely just by you moving your body. Just consider all that your mind has to do as you complete some of the simplest activities that we do every day without ever thinking about it. "Even a simple movement like reaching out to pick up a glass of water can be a complex motor task to study. Not only does your brain have to figure out which muscles to contract and in which order to steer your hand to the glass, it also has to estimate the force needed to pick up the glass. Other factors, like how much water is in the glass and what material the glass is made from, also influence the brain's calculations."[3]

So you see, even doing something as simple as going to get a glass of water during a time of temptation is sometimes enough (when coupled with immediate prayer as discussed in the previous chapter) to seriously diminish or even end the current temptation completely. I mean, how long does it take to say, "Lord, help me. I'm facing temptation. Please protect me and help me make wise choices" and then get up and leave the room, or turn off that television or computer and get out of your chair? I'm suggesting about thirty seconds to do both of those, but I suppose it depends on how fast you walk to get out that room, or whether or not you can find the TV remote; but you get my point. Trust me, I've done it many times, and it works. So when you're tempted to act out in some fashion, and prayer alone was not enough to diminish its pull on you, don't just do nothing; get moving and get your brain working on something else.

OK, I'm Moving; Now What?

Alright, Guy, you've got me doing the Steve Martin shimmy all over the place and I look like an idiot; now what? Well, first of all, do everyone a favor and stop shaking your shoulders like that before someone thinks you're having a seizure and dials 911. Often, as I just said, moving to another room, getting a drink of water, crossing the street or quickly going up and down a set of stairs is enough to suspend the temptation. But let's expand on this a little and go beyond our sixty-second Tempt-Away plan. It's often not enough to move our bodies on purpose; we need to move our bodies *for a purpose*.

The Worst Restaurant in the World

I have found it helpful to look at our responses to temptation in much the same way as we would look at a menu in a restaurant. What if you went into a local diner and upon opening up the menu discovered that they only offered one item to choose from? One choice: the burger; a burger for breakfast, a burger for lunch, a burger for dinner and that same burger for dessert. Well, actually, if you're like my seventeen-year-old son who only orders burgers no matter what restaurant we go into, you'd be thrilled, but most of us would choose another place to eat. When you go to a diner, you want choice and variety; you may even prefer a cafeteria or an all-you-can-eat buffet (now we're talking!) where there is a smorgasbord of foods to pick and choose from.

When it comes to temptation, one of the reasons why we often end up failing the test is that we have not planned and prepared other options beforehand; we've not added a variety of activities to our menu, so when enticement to sin arrives, we think we have only one choice we can make, and that is to give in to the temptation. But what if you deliberately took the time to prepare and wrote down a list of alternative activities that you could quickly turn to instead of the sinful action that you were being tempted with?

What Do You Really Enjoy Doing?

Think about what you really enjoy doing. Love Stephen King novels? Then get his latest book of horror and put it out where you can easily and quickly get to it, and when the lure of sin hits you, offer your quick prayer (Step 1), and then get moving. Move your body to your copy of *Pet Cemetery* and divert your energies and attention into being scared silly. Maybe you love listening to music; then have your favorite playlist ready to go. It could be you enjoy baking; then have the ingredients in your cupboard, ready for such an eventuality, and get making those cookies. How about shooting hoops in the driveway, or if you're Canadian like me, taking some shots at the net? Perhaps you have a favorite hobby that gets your mojo going like gardening, sewing, restoring an old car, writing, painting or even shopping. It could be you're in the middle of *Downton Abbey* and you can't wait to see who dies next. Of course, strenuous physical activity also works great.

Whatever it is, just ensure that it is an activity that is moving you away from the temptation, not something that could only entice you further. For instance, if you're facing the temptation to look at inappropriate or sinful websites on your computer, then using your Mac to watch a movie or browse through Facebook is probably not the best choice; choose another menu item.

Even Scripture encourages us to find alternative activities to acting out in sin, doing something purposeful as opposed to just resisting temptation. The suggestion offered by the apostle Paul on what to do in place of committing a sinful action is awesome: Galatians 5:13 says, "You, my brothers and sisters, were called to be free. But do not use your freedom to indulge the flesh; rather, serve one another humbly in love."

Serving. What an amazing idea! During times of temptation, is there a more selfish, self-centered, egocentric, and self-indulgent moment of our day? I don't think so. Temptation is all about getting our own personal needs met, no matter what the cost, regardless of whom it hurts. Paul calls us to take our eyes off ourselves and to focus on meeting the needs of others. What a brilliant move! Are you facing temptation? Pray, then get up and serve someone. Paul says in Galatians 6:10, "Therefore, as we have opportunity, let us do good to all people, especially to those who belong to the family of believers."

Take your eyes off yourself and put them on someone else who could use some help. This can be as simple as cleaning up some dirty dishes (even if they're not yours), cutting the grass, straightening up a room or calling or visiting someone who could use some encouragement. I even heard of a man who, upon facing temptation, would have at the ready (he was prepared) a pen and notepaper. He would focus on others by writing encouraging notes to people at his church and then would hand them out at the next Sunday morning worship service. Everyone felt blessed by this gesture of kindness, and this gentleman was able to consistently overcome the enticement of sin, partly because he had planned and prepared by putting another item on his menu to choose from when it was needed.

Danger: No Trespassing!

So far we've talked about the importance of movement in our ability to affect how the brain works. We've discussed how necessary it is to actually move so that we are taking ourselves away from the thing that is tempting us. We've talked about how we need to move on purpose, for a purpose. Finally I want us to talk about the bigger picture: the importance of movement in regard to the trajectory of our lives overall.

The question I want you to think about is this: do you live a life that has you consistently moving closer to sin, or farther away from it? Don't answer too quickly! It can be tricky to spot such a thing in our own lives. It's not that obvious sometimes. As Jeremiah 17:9 so correctly says, "The heart is deceitful above all things and beyond cure. Who can understand it?"

At the expense of my children maybe needing to seek a shrink of their own someday because their father kept using them as examples in his books, let me tell you a true story about my oldest son. Halifax, Nova Scotia is a military city on Canada's east coast. Canada's Atlantic navy is stationed and headquartered there, which means that the city has several military bases, shooting ranges, armor depots and the like. Yes, Canada has a proud army, air force and navy. It's not that big, mind you, especially for a country as large as Canada, but when you live next door to a nation that is a friend and ally and who also happens to have the most powerful and largest military in the history of the world, you don't really need a huge fighting force. Sometimes we even put bullets in our guns, and on the rarest of occasions, our submarine will even go under water!

One summer day back when my oldest son (who is now in his twenties) was around sixteen years old, he and his best friend travelled by city bus to a part of town they were not familiar with. Not having planned properly, they left home without enough money to take a bus both there and back and have lunch, which meant they ended up stranded on the far side of town without a way home, except to put one foot in front of the other. Granted, Halifax is not New York City, but it was still quite a distance for them to hike. Of course, they tried calling their parents to beg for a ride, but for whatever reason, we didn't get their anxious pleas for help. (It's also highly likely that I did, but I figured they're young and it's summer, and they need to learn a lesson, so walking home wouldn't kill them—little did I know!)

So, they started the long journey home like two vagrant wanderers. As they travelled they came upon a huge field that was surrounded by a chain link fence. One of them (my son, I'm sure) came up with the brilliant idea that they could cut down their distance by hopping the fence and going through this protected piece of property. So, over they went. As they were trespassing, they decided to stop and eat what they had purchased for lunch. So there they sat, under the glorious sun, eating away and no doubt telling one another their dopey stories and jokes to pass the time. When their stomachs were full of Coke, Doritos and Skittles, the official lunch of all sixteen-year-old boys on a hot summer day, they continued on to the other side of the property and climbed the fence to get out. Upon jumping down the other side, they turned to see a huge sign attached to the barrier they had just crawled over that read: "DANGER. NO TRESSPASSING! MILITARY FIRING RANGE. UNEXPLOADED SHELLS." I still shake my head in disbelief.

These two geniuses started a chain of events that could have ultimately gotten them picked up by military police, seriously injured or even possibly killed, all because they didn't plan properly, count the cost or consider the consequences of their decisions. They made one bad choice after another that were all linked together and could have resulted in a catastrophe, as opposed to a funny story they will tell their kids someday. We've all been there, right? Maybe not trespassing through a military firing range, but we've all been guilty of putting into effect a chain of events that took us to places we shouldn't be; my son's dad included. If only we could recognize the perils along the way, long before we're actually in danger. If only we could break the chain of events early enough so that we could be saved from all of the hurt and damage of a crash!

Breaking the Chain

Let's begin by unpacking a story in Genesis that is an excellent example of how easily one can move in the wrong direction with their lives by making poor choices, not planning properly and not considering the consequences of their decisions. I want us to look at the story of Lot, Abram's nephew.

By way of setting up the scene, Abram and Lot were both wealthy men and had big families, large herds and plenty of possessions. By the time we get to Genesis 13, both families had been traveling, looking for a new place to settle. They eventually stopped at a place between Bethel and Ai. The area, however, was apparently not abundant enough to support both clans, and eventually there were arguments between the two families and their farmers. Abram wanted peace, so he told Lot that he was free to take his family, possessions, flocks and herds in any direction he chose.

> So Abram said to Lot, "Let's not have any quarreling between you and me, or between your herders and mine, for we are close relatives. Is not the whole land before you? Let's part company. If you go to the left, I'll go to the right; if you go to the right, I'll go to the left."

> Lot looked around and saw that the whole plain of the
> Jordan toward Zoar was well watered, like the garden of
> the LORD, like the land of Egypt. (This was before the LORD
> destroyed Sodom and Gomorrah.) So Lot chose for himself the
> whole plain of the Jordan and set out toward the east. The two
> men parted company: Abram lived in the land of Canaan, while
> Lot lived among the cities of the plain and pitched his tents
> near Sodom. Now the people of Sodom were wicked and were
> sinning greatly against the LORD. (Genesis 13:8–13)

To see the consequences of Lot's terrible decision-making and witness the chain of events that led to his downfall, let us go to the next chapter, Genesis 14:8–9 and 11–12:

> Then the king of Sodom, the king of Gomorrah, the king
> of Admah, the king of Zeboiim and the king of Bela (that is,
> Zoar) marched out and drew up their battle lines in the Valley of
> Siddim against Kedorlaomer king of Elam, Tidal king of Goiim,
> Amraphel king of Shinar and Arioch king of Ellasar—four kings
> against five... The four kings seized all the goods of Sodom and
> Gomorrah and all their food; then they went away. They also
> carried off Abram's nephew Lot and his possessions, since he
> was living in Sodom.

As you read through this train wreck of a story, otherwise known as Lot's life, it's easy to see with 20/20 hindsight how the man could have avoided the horrific consequences and simply broken the chain of events that he encountered along the way. Lot had several opportunities to save himself and his family, but he just kept moving in the wrong direction, and with each terrible decision seemed determined to draw only closer to his demise, not farther from it.

Remember, at any point along this storyline, Lot could have put a stop to the madness.

Chain Link #1: Lot and Abram quarrel and separate—Genesis 13:8–11. What if Lot and Abram had worked out their differences instead of separating? What if they had reasoned with one another and been determined to come up with a solution? Unresolved situations where there are hard feelings and no reconciliation always lead to more sin. Disunity, arguments, fighting, and unsettled issues between loved ones and even fellow Christians always are a fast and slippery slope downward. If only Abram and Lot had talked to work things out. If only they had apologized for the fighting and had stayed together, the chain would have been broken.

Chain Link #2: Lot "looked around and saw" the valley of Sodom—Genesis 13:10. All that glitters is not gold. It's funny how Lot looked around and saw all the benefits of the land before him but somehow was able to ignore the dangers of choosing the area where Sodom was located. Lot would have known about this city, that it was full of people who "were wicked and were sinning greatly against the Lord." What if Lot had not allowed his lust for greener pastures to override his spiritual convictions? What if he had been courageous enough to admit to himself that living in the land with these wicked people made it not worth choosing the area, no matter how green and well-watered the land was? Lot could have broken the chain right then and there, but no; the guy just kept going.

Satan loves to masquerade as an angel of light (2 Corinthians 11:14). He's an expert at selling us things that look amazing, alluring and beautiful, while cleverly hiding the dangers and pitfalls that lurk in the background. Like Lot, we're often well aware of the dangers that lie ahead; we're not completely stupid, right? It's just that the benefits look so great that we think we can have our cake and eat it too. We think we can get close to sin without burning ourselves.

But we cannot! As it says in Proverbs 6:27–29:

> *Can a man scoop fire into his lap*
> *without his clothes being burned?*
> *Can a man walk on hot coals*
> *without his feet being scorched?*
> *So is he who sleeps with another man's wife;*
> *no one who touches her will go unpunished.*

I don't care how beautiful the other man's wife may be! The consequences of sleeping with her will be life altering for all involved. Satan does not want us to see the painful consequences of our sinful choices, only the fun and enjoyment we may experience momentarily before the full weight of our actions sets in.

Chain Link #3: Lot "set out toward" Sodom—Genesis 13:11. We need to be careful of the trajectory of our life. I'll be honest. I know whether watching a certain show or movie will eventually cause me grief. I know what kinds of conversations will soon turn gossipy slanderous if I'm not careful. I know what emotions left unchecked will get me to ultimately sin if I stay focused on them. I may not be the brightest light in the harbor, but I'm no dummy. Lot was no dummy either; he knew that the evil city of Sodom was in this direction, yet he went towards it anyway. He deliberately and purposefully moved himself and, even more shockingly, his family into danger. What if he had stopped in his tracks and turned around and gone back to Abram? What if he had veered in another direction? He could have still stopped the craziness and broken the chain of events, avoiding the crash, but no; he kept going. Believing the lie that he could live close to the sin and not sin himself was devastating.

Chain Link #4: Lot "pitched his tents near" Sodom—Genesis 13:12. Even at this point, Lot still could have broken the chain, after he had separated from Abram, after he saw and set out toward the evil city, had he come to his senses and simply refused to pitch his tent so close to the filth and wretchedness of that city. But no; he stopped, unpacked and set up his home with his wives and his children and his loved ones, right next door to the danger. Thanks for that, Dad.

Chain Link #5: Lot "was living in" Sodom—Genesis 14:12. And here's the granddaddy of them all: by the time we get to chapter 14, Lot is no longer "near"; he's actually now "in" the middle of it all!

Notice the slow but steady progression that led to the crash of this man's life:

1. Lot separated from Abram because of unresolved fighting and arguing.
2. He saw Sodom.
3. He set out toward Sodom.
4. He pitched his tent near Sodom.
5. Then he lived in Sodom.
6. Finally, we read of him being taken captive in battle.

These can be our steps to destruction as well. We separate from fellowship. We allow hurt feelings to come between us and other

Christians, between us and our spouse and even sometimes between us and God. We see something sinful, a thing we want because we believe it will make us happy or fulfilled, and so we focus on it. We fantasize about it. We set out toward it. We pitch our tent near it. We live in it and finally are taken captive by it.

Lot, however, was in good company. King David was also self-deceived and painfully unaware of how his spiritual dullness slowly but surely moved him in a dangerous direction that led to the biggest downfall of his life. 2 Samuel 11:1–5 records this crash for us:

> In the spring, at the time when kings go off to war, David sent Joab out with the king's men and the whole Israelite army. They destroyed the Ammonites and besieged Rabbah. But David remained in Jerusalem.
>
> One evening David got up from his bed and walked around on the roof of the palace. From the roof he saw a woman bathing. The woman was very beautiful, and David sent someone to find out about her. The man said, "She is Bathsheba, the daughter of Eliam and the wife of Uriah the Hittite." Then David sent messengers to get her. She came to him, and he slept with her. (Now she was purifying herself from her monthly uncleanness.) Then she went back home. The woman conceived and sent word to David, saying, "I am pregnant."

And then, right when you think things couldn't possibly get worse, the author of 2 Samuel records that it indeed can!

> In the morning David wrote a letter to Joab and sent it with Uriah. In it he wrote, "Put Uriah out in front where the fighting is fiercest. Then withdraw from him so he will be struck down and die."
>
> So while Joab had the city under siege, he put Uriah at a place where he knew the strongest defenders were. When the men of the city came out and fought against Joab, some of the men in David's army fell; moreover, Uriah the Hittite died.
> (2 Samuel 11:14–17)

Just look at the links that combined to create a chain of events that ultimately caused this disaster:

Chain Link #1: When Kings go off to war, David stayed home. He didn't recognize that boredom is not healthy and done something about it, but no; he decided to keep moving in a bad direction.

Chain Link #2: When David saw a woman bathing from his rooftop, he should have run inside immediately, but he obviously stayed out on the balcony to spy on her in lust.

Chain Link #3: When David learned that she was a married woman, he most certainly should have dropped the issue, but instead, he sent a messenger to go and bring her to him.

Chain Link #4: Upon meeting her in person, things had reached a feverish point of no return. David had sex with the woman.

Chain Link #5: And finally, he still had an opportunity to cut the terrible chain of events by confessing adultery, repenting and leaving the woman alone, but instead, he only escalated his sin and damage to everyone around him by having Bathsheba's husband murdered.

What are the links that can often send my life moving in the wrong direction to an ultimate crash? I get tired and think I deserve a rest; I miss prayer and Bible study because I am so "busy." I feel overwhelmed with responsibility, or I look at my bills or an area in my life that I feel like I am failing at and focus on it. I start feeling sorry for myself and get into self-pity. I want to be left alone, so I pull back emotionally from those closest to me. I begin to believe that I deserve to feel better than I do, and Satan is right there to make sure that there are many options available. And before you know it I'm off and running, right towards the sin. In the series of events that have led to the crashes in my life, there were always opportunities to take an exit ramp, to cut the chain of events that could lead to my downfall, but I'm afraid I'm sometimes too much like Lot and King David. As it says in James 1:14–15, "Each person is tempted when they are dragged away by their own evil desire and enticed. Then, after desire has conceived, it gives birth to sin; and sin, when it is full-grown, gives birth to death."

To be successful in overcoming temptation, you've got to be alert and honest with yourself and others. You must be able to see with spiritual eyes what is occurring and then remove one of the links that is leading you down the path to destruction. You must live your spiritual life on purpose, deliberately. I love Peter's call for us to have minds that are alert and fully sober. When my mind is fuzzy and dull, I can always be sure that trouble is nearby. Remember the quote near the beginning of this chapter by Steve Sisgold, the body management therapist, about how we can easily become "fuzzy and confused" and therefore stuck in some kind of unproductive activity? Was Mr. Sisgold referring to sin? I don't think so. But I certainly am, and so is Peter:

> *Therefore, with minds that are alert and fully sober, set your hope on the grace to be brought to you when Jesus Christ is revealed at his coming. As obedient children, do not conform to the evil desires you had when you lived in ignorance. But just as he who called you is holy, so be holy in all you do; for it is written: "Be holy, because I am holy."*
>
> *Since you call on a Father who judges each person's work impartially, live out your time as foreigners here in reverent fear.* (1 Peter 1:13–17)

Do you see in this passage the call by Peter for us to live our lives "on purpose?" How about this from Paul:

> *Do you not know that in a race all the runners run, but only one gets the prize? Run in such a way as to get the prize. Everyone who competes in the games goes into strict training. They do it to get a crown that will not last, but we do it to get a crown that will last forever. Therefore I do not run like someone running aimlessly; I do not fight like a boxer beating the air. No, I strike a blow to my body and make it my slave so that after I have preached to others, I myself will not be disqualified for the prize.* (1 Corinthians 9:24–27)

And so that is Step 2 of the Tempt-Away plan on how to defeat every temptation you face in less than sixty seconds.

Step 1: Pray. 15 seconds

Step 2: Move. 15 seconds

If, after praying and physically moving your body away from the temptation or at least to distract your mind and attention, you still feel temptation to sin, then it's time to intensify your attempts to Step 3 of the Tempt-Away plan.

Small Group Discussion Questions

1. Have you ever experienced that by moving your body, you were able to refocus your mind on something else, helping you overcome temptation?

2. How does unresolved conflict lead us down a path of sin? Can you share a personal example?

3. In what ways can you relate to Lot or David?

4. What are some of the chain links that send our lives moving in the wrong direction to an ultimate crash? What are some choices we can make to break the chain at any link?

5. How will this chapter help you to live your spiritual life "on purpose"?

End Notes:

1. "Neuroscience." Psychology Today. N.d. https://www. psychologytoday.com/basics/neuroscience.

2. Sisgold, Steve. "Change Your Movement, Change Your Brain." 22 Oct. 2014. https://www.psychologytoday.com/blog/life-in-body/201410/ change-your-movement-change-your-brain.

3. Schwerin, Susan, PhD. "The Anatomy of Movement." Brain Connection. 5 Mar. 2013. http://brainconnection.brainhq. com/2013/03/05/the-anatomy-of-movement.

Chapter Four

Sweat the Small Stuff

*I want to be a jerk like the rest of my friends,
and have fun and not care about the consequences,
but I just can't, now.*   —Leonardo DiCaprio

On August 14, 2003, at 3:32 p.m. a series of small, seemingly insignificant events collided, initiating a chain reaction that quickly affected the lives of an estimated 50 million people in two countries, costing billions of dollars in economic losses and eleven deaths. It was the largest electrical blackout in North American history. What was the cause of the catastrophe? Being on the heels of 9/11 had many fearing that it was terrorism. Thankfully that was not the case. Conspiracy theorists blamed the U.S. government, claiming that it was conducting secret military experiments. However, according to the official report released almost five years later, the real truth was much less sinister. A local power company had neglected to trim trees near its high-voltage lines. When the weather is hot and power is in high demand, the lines droop. Three lines in the Cincinnati area sagged so low that they touched tree branches, creating short circuits that took the lines out of service. Many have suggested that squirrels could even be partially blamed as they ran back and forth along the power lines forcing them to touch the trees, as this does occasionally occur.

Alarms at the control room of the power company should have alerted those who were monitoring the controls that day, but the alarm system was not working due to a bug in the system, so technicians did not know of the shorted-out lines. A backup alarm system in the Midwest was supposed to have a computer program in place to monitor power flows and should have caught this glitch, but the technician had shut the system off to upgrade the software, and then went to lunch forgetting to turn it back on again. The domino effect began. "Automatic relays (basically industrial-scale circuit breakers) were programmed to protect equipment, not to ride out any disturbance, and as each one acted, isolating a power line or a transformer, the disturbance got bigger and bigger, until a huge house of cards collapsed."[1] The result was the second-largest electrical blackout in the world, sending the entire northeastern part of the United States and the province of Ontario, Canada into the dark.

Chaos Everywhere!

Electricity is taken for granted until you don't have it. Thousands of commuters were stuck in underground subway trains in both New York City and Toronto forcing men, women and children to walk along the tracks in the dark to find exits leading them to daylight. People were left stranded in skyscraper elevators. Hundreds of thousands of office workers in affected cities flooded the streets looking for a way to get home, but traffic had come to a complete halt, causing gridlock everywhere, meaning that throngs of people trudged on foot as downtown cores were evacuated. People abandoned cars, leaving them in the middle of the street. Trains were not running. Major international airports like JFK, LaGuardia and Newark Liberty in the New York area, Pearson International in Toronto and Detroit International cancelled all flights, causing flight interruptions globally. Most cities' water supplies ran on electrical pumps, meaning that the only way for water to get from local lakes to the tap was with electrical power. Most metropolitan areas had only a few hours of water available for their citizens, causing fears of possible health and safety issues. As night fell, looting in some areas ensued. Hotels were left having their guests sleep in their front lobbies as staff handed out blankets, pillows and water.

Some cities had to wait almost three days. In most affected areas, the power was out for twenty-nine hours. In that time period, in New York City alone, over 3,000 fire calls were reported as people started using candles for light. Emergency services had to respond to over 80,000 emergency 911 calls, more than double the average.

I can recall those days easily. My family and I lived in Toronto at the time, and my wife and I were responsible for purchasing all of the food for a weekend teen camp that our local church was about to host. We had come home after buying enough food to feed a small army and had just unloaded it all into our air-conditioned basement to keep things cool, but suddenly the air conditioning was gone and the temperature quickly started rising. Luckily, the power came back on before anything went bad and the camp went on as planned.

Throughout the blackout, my children were quite elated, as a local ice cream store started giving away free cones and ice cream sundaes in order to dispose of their product before all of it melted. My kids were more than happy to assist them in this endeavor, only out of concern, of course. I also remember our family all crowding into our car for some air-conditioned relief and so that mom and dad could listen to the radio for news reports on what was happening in the outside world. For those two evenings, our neighborhood had quite a festive mood as most people did not have to work, and at night it turned into somewhat of a street party as neighbors came out to mill about and visit with one another and do something they hadn't been able to do in decades: look at the stars. The Milky Way became visible to the naked eye, something impossible in a major metropolitan area when the electricity is working.

When the power came back on, life went back to normal, of course. The neighbors went back to keeping to themselves, the street parties ended, the stars disappeared again, and ice cream cones went back to being $1.25 a scoop.

The point to sharing all of this is to remind us how a few small, seemingly insignificant events can converge to create one gargantuan dilemma affecting many. In the case of the great blackout of 2003, it was some untrimmed tree branches, some low-swinging power lines, a couple of squirrels, an alarm that didn't work and a guy who shut down the backup system for a few minutes, but then forgot to turn it back on when he went to go have his meatball sub. Throw it all together, and what do you have? Fifty million people wandering around in the dark bumping into each other, 6.1 billion dollars in financial losses and eleven deaths.

Maybe We *Should* Sweat the Small Stuff

In Chapter One I stated that temptation should be considered the most exciting part of your day because it gives you the opportunity to show God whom you have decided to follow. Can I add that temptation is also the most dangerous part of your day? There's no such thing as a small temptation. Temptation, like a squirrel running along a power line in Cleveland, while seemingly insignificant, if not dealt with instantly has the *potential* to cause the largest spiritual blackout in the history of your life. Temptation will shipwreck a life faster than the Titanic hitting an iceberg!

Think I'm overstating things? Every marriage that has ended in divorce can have their troubles traced back to an initial temptation, and most often a small one at that, by either one or both parties. Every person you know who has had their life destroyed by drugs, alcohol or illicit sex had their problems start with a simple temptation. Temptation left unchecked has ruined entire careers, wiped out personal wealth and demolished political futures.

Some of the most damaging and hurtful things I have ever done in my life to other people or to myself, actions or words that have caused years of pain and insecurity, started with a simple thought. Some of the most painful things that people have ever done to me started as a small temptation.

A man molested me when I was eight years old. I never spoke of it until I was in my mid-thirties. I can't know for certain what was going through this man's mind at the time, but I do believe that if he had stopped to consider the consequences of what it was he was about to do, if he had just paused long enough to contemplate the ramifications of what this would do to my life and his, it would have given him time to stop himself and save both of us years of pain and shame and regret. There is no such thing as a small temptation. They all start small, and some of them can initiate a chain reaction that can ruin your life and that of others.

Tempt-Away Step 3: Consider the Consequences

And so this leads us to the third step of the Tempt-Away plan to defeat every temptation you face in less than sixty seconds: consider the consequences. Temptation has arrived, you've said a quick prayer, you've moved out of the situation (and even on to doing something more productive like serving someone). If temptation still is hounding you, what you must do now is stop and think, just for a matter of seconds, what consequences you or others will face if you act out as you are being tempted to do. Take a moment to consider.

Life can come at you pretty quickly, especially when it involves temptation. I think it's one of Satan's ploys to trick us into sin—that we wouldn't have time to stop and think. When this happens to me, the strategy of slowing things down so that I can pause and consider the consequences of what it is I want to do has saved me from saying and doing many dumb things that would only cause chaos in my life.

For instance, when someone cuts me off on the highway or verbally attacks me or falsely accuses me of something, it can be easy for me to go from zero to sixty pretty quickly. I'm not proud of that fact, but that's me. I've learned that I have to force my mind to pause and consider, "Is this blockhead who almost ran me off the road worth becoming angry over? Will I give him that much power in my life? I don't like it when I'm enraged; I don't like how it feels; it can ruin my day and even lead to other sins. So no, I will calm myself and not give the situation this much influence in my life. I choose to stay calm." I've had to have that talk with myself many times, and it works. It only takes five seconds to mentally go through that thought process, but it's enough time for me to slow things down and consider whether I will fly off the handle and become a jerk myself, or whether I will act like Christ and stay calm.

The Biggest Fight We've Ever Had

The biggest fight my wife and I ever had was in the parking lot of Shell Factory ("Southwest Florida's #1 destination for seashells") in Fort Myers in front of gawking local shoppers.

The battle occurred one week after our wedding in February 1991. The nuptials took place in Toronto, but we honeymooned in Florida to escape the Canadian winter. I didn't budget properly (like father, like son, apparently) and by the end of the first week, we were thousands of miles away from home with little money. That left us staying in cheap motels that no bride should ever have to sleep in, and surviving off the value menus at restaurants where you get to color the menu. Can I show a girl a good time, or what?

One day as we were driving past the amusement parks and attractions that we couldn't afford to get into, I saw a massive sign welcoming us to Shell Factory. Being that gift-giving is my love language, I had wanted to buy some souvenirs for family and friends up north. Shell Factory seemed like the perfect place. I promised my bride that due to the fact that we were practically broke, I would be careful and purchase just a few items, but when we entered the massive warehouse emporium of seashells, trinkets and gifts, the redneck inside of me just came alive! There were seashell key chains, seashell earrings, seashell lamps, seashell hats, seashell snow globes, seashell necklaces, seashell bracelets, seashell picture frames, seashell steering wheels, seashell watches, seashell pottery items, seashell coffee mugs, seashell everything! And, oh yeah, they had plain ole seashells, too, and not just from Florida, but from all over the world. It was quite an amazing place!

While Cathy picked up a few small items totaling a few dollars, I gleefully jam-packed a shopping cart full of beautiful mementos that I just knew everyone back in Canada would proudly display on their fireplace mantels. When I got to the cash register, my newlywed wife's facial features looked odd to me, like they were somehow contorted, though I couldn't put my finger on quite why. She wasn't saying anything, so I figured that was a good sign.

Apparently that is not a good sign, or so I have learned over the years. As I was loading up the trunk of our rental with the bags of everything seashell, that beautiful, kind, sweet, genteel woman that had lovingly said "I do" only seven days earlier turned into this creature I had never seen before. She exploded! She was angry, I felt attacked (how could she not want to buy gifts for our loved ones? How selfish!), and before we knew it, it was show time! The new Mr. and Mrs. Hammond were off and running and having their first big fight in the parking lot of Shell Factory; and it was a doozy! I'm sure the event left both of us feeling like the wedding was a mistake. What had we done? Love may be blind, but marriage is a real eye-opener! The next four hours we drove in complete silence across Alligator

Alley toward Fort Lauderdale except for the few tentative attempts I made to make her laugh at the situation. Apparently laughing was not in the cards that day, or for the next couple of days! We had decided before the wedding that we would never go to bed angry, which means we didn't sleep for the rest of that week. Marriages are made in heaven, but so are lightning and thunder! Fortunately, it was the last fight like that we've ever had. Certainly we've had our disagreements over the years, but the first rumble was so unpleasant, I think we decided we just didn't want to go for round two. We're just about to celebrate our twenty-fifth year together, and it's been the best fifteen years of my life! (The first ten were somewhat challenging.)

The Power of the Tongue

It's amazing how words and comments and little jabs, or even full-out verbal punches, can come out of our mouths and hurt the people we love the most, isn't it? James bluntly tells us the truth about the power of the tongue:

> *When we put bits into the mouths of horses to make them obey us, we can turn the whole animal. Or take ships as an example. Although they are so large and are driven by strong winds, they are steered by a very small rudder wherever the pilot wants to go. Likewise, the tongue is a small part of the body, but it makes great boasts. Consider what a great forest is set on fire by a small spark. The tongue also is a fire, a world of evil among the parts of the body. It corrupts the whole body, sets the whole course of one's life on fire, and is itself set on fire by hell.*
>
> *All kinds of animals, birds, reptiles and sea creatures are being tamed and have been tamed by mankind, but no human being can tame the tongue. It is a restless evil, full of deadly poison.* (James 3:3–8)

[handwritten marginal note: *You control where you steer that boat*]

And then, just to make sure that we really got the point, he says in verses 9 and 10, "With the tongue we praise our Lord and Father, and with it we curse human beings, who have been made in God's likeness. Out of the same mouth come praise and cursing. My brothers and sisters, this should not be."

Husbands and wives, if there's ever a time to stop and consider the consequences, it is when you are speaking with your spouse when tensions are high. Every time you are tempted to say something that is cutting, unkind or disrespectful, you've got to stop yourself. Literally shut your mouth, leave the room and cool your jets before you speak again. Do not curse your lifelong companion with the same mouth you just praised God with at church on Sunday. Consider the consequences. Quickly ask yourself, is it worth it for me to lash out in anger? How will I feel after I say the things I'm tempted to? How will it make my spouse feel? Will it improve the situation or solve the problem? This could lead to hours or even days (or longer) of hurt and resentment and me being on the couch. Count the cost before you say another syllable. If you need to, leave the room and go pray, and take time to cool down before addressing the problem.

Are those mean words worth it?

Plan Ahead *Then don't say (or think) them!*

One helpful spousal strategy is to plan ahead. Temptation may come on you like a whirlwind, but if you've planned ahead for this eventuality, you'll obviously be more prepared. You know yourself well and you know how you'll be tempted to respond when things escalate at home. The time to figure out how to respond righteously is not when she's holding the frying pan above her head, but before, when things are calm. So stop and consider how you will behave long before you get into this situation so that you don't just react.

In fact, no matter what the temptation, planning ahead is always a good idea. For some strange reason, most of us fail at doing this. We plan for everything else in life; we plan our schedules; we plan our school work; we plan how we'll get the job done; we plan what we will wear and what top matches what skirt; we plan what we will watch on television and what we will record so that we can watch it later; we plan on who we will call, text, Facebook, Instagram, tweet and email; we plan our finances; we plan what groceries we will buy; we plan what bus we will take; we plan our vacations—the list goes on and on. But for some reason most of us put little or no thought into the one thing that we absolutely and most definitely know we will face several times a day: we don't plan our response to temptation.

There's more to overcoming the allurement of sin than just white-knuckling it through life. There's more to defeating temptation than

We Plan for so many things during the day so why can't we will overcome temptation

just saying no. That kind of self-sacrifice in the name of obedience to God is helpful because it will at times keep you away from sin, but to live month after month, year after year of just saying no because you're trying not to sin is not a very spiritually mature way of dealing with your temptations. If you were to hold a single piece of paper above your head and keep it there for a long period of time, eventually your arm would get tired. You could be as determined as you want to keep that piece of paper above your head, but eventually your arm would have to come down. That is what it is like when we attack temptation through determination alone. It works for a while, but eventually you'll tire out and won't be able to continue.

Remember what we discussed in Chapter One: the ultimate goal of our lives is not to stop sinning; it is to love God. Self-denial for the sake of self-denial may indeed help you to overcome temptation, but it does nothing in regard to helping you know your heavenly Father in a deeper and more intimate way, it does not help you rely on him for your strength and sustenance, and it does not leave you relying on the word of God for encouragement.

Ephesians 4:22–24 says: ↳ *Ask God to help You overcome that temptation*

You were taught, with regard to your former way of life, to put off your old self, which is being corrupted by its deceitful desires; to be made new in the attitude of your minds; and to put on the new self, created to be like God in true righteousness and holiness.

Mind transformation doesn't happen by accident, and it doesn't happen overnight. It takes an understanding of the fact that this kind of evolution requires a lifelong commitment and a maturity that is willing to be unrelenting in its pursuit, while also agonizingly patient as one tries, stumbles and rises again to keep moving forward.

So, with that said, it's a helpful suggestion to choose a few short scriptures that you can memorize or even carry with you on your cellphone for easy access, passages that will help you in your time of need. Since no one knows your own areas of weakness better than you, sit down with a Bible and pre-select some scriptures that will assist you when Satan whispers. Plan ahead:

- You know the kind of gossip that regularly occurs when you speak with that certain friend; it's what this relationship seems to be built on. However, it's been bothering you that you gossip like this, and you want to stop slandering others and betraying their confidence. The consequence of your gossip has been that you have felt the pang in your heart every time it's occurred knowing that you just broke someone's trust and even snickered at his or her plight, so you want to change. Good for you! You have a lunch scheduled with this individual and you know that the temptation to gossip about others will be prevalent. What should you do? Follow the Tempt-Away steps when you meet, but also, plan ahead. Write out or memorize Proverbs 11:13: "A gossip betrays a confidence, but a trustworthy person keeps a secret" and be prepared.

- You know the lustful thoughts and fantasies that you are tempted to have when you are around that particular woman at work. The consequence of this is that your lust has been degrading to this woman, even though she is not aware of what you've been doing, and if you're married, you certainly have been causing harm to your relationship with your wife. But this is a work environment, and you know you will see this woman at work tomorrow. How will you handle this? Follow the Tempt-Away steps when you're tempted to sin like this again, but also plan ahead. Memorize or have handy scriptures like Job 31:1: "I made a covenant with my eyes not to look lustfully at a young woman" and be prepared.

- You know the kind of filthy language that is easy for you to use when you hang around that certain group of friends at school. It bothers you every time you curse and tell those crude jokes, but you've been unable to stop. It's just the way everyone talks, and it's what you do to fit in. What should you do? Well, besides maybe looking for some new friends, I'd suggest you memorize Ephesians 5:4 and be prepared: "Nor should there be obscenity, foolish talk or coarse joking, which are out of place, but rather thanksgiving" and then use the Tempt-Away plan if you're tempted to act out in this way.

- You know how easy it is for you to slip into a mode where you are critical and judgmental of others. When people don't do things the way you think they should be done, when others don't live up to your standards, or when people don't do what you ask, it's easy for you to have a critical and judgmental spirit. It is a struggle, and you know that it is damaging to your relationship with God and with people you love. What should you do? When you feel the urge to be critical, follow the Tempt-Away steps, but also memorize, along with other scriptures, James 2:13 and quote it to yourself when you need it: "Judgment without mercy will be shown to anyone who has not been merciful. Mercy triumphs over judgment."

The Big Letdown

I love Coke. It's the most recognized and popular drink on the planet for a reason: it tastes great. On a hot summer day there's nothing better than ice cold Coca-Cola. Since its inception, the company has had a brilliant marketing strategy using a long list of slogans that have gone beyond simply advertising a product, but have also become part of pop culture. Probably the three most popular Coke jingles of all time are "Things go better with Coke" from 1963; "It's the real thing" from 1969 and the most famous of all, "Have a Coke and a smile" from 1979, a slogan that took off largely due to a television commercial that aired during the 1980 Super Bowl. It starred Pittsburgh Steelers defensive tackle "Mean Joe" Green as he limped off the field after a game. Some kid comes up to the football superstar and offers him his bottle of Coke, which Mean Joe guzzles down. As the kid turns away to leave, Green says, "Hey kid, catch!" and throws him his game-worn jersey while the song in the background plays: "A coke and a smile makes me feel good, makes me feel nice. That's the way it should be; I like to see the whole world smiling with me. Coca-Cola adds life. Have a Coke and a smile!"

I just YouTubed that commercial to watch it as I was writing this out and I've got to admit, my eyes got misty watching it again all these years later. That commercial was shown over and over again, not just in North America, but across Europe, too. It won the Clio Award (the international advertising industry's top prize) for the best television commercial in 1980 and was listed by *TV Guide* as one of the top ten television commercials of all time.

So the jingle is catchy and the drink tastes amazing, but it's no secret that soft drinks in general aren't good for us. They may be fine to consume in moderation, but you don't need to be a licensed dietician to know that a steady diet of any brew that is full of high fructose corn syrup, caffeine, phosphoric acid, sodium benzoate and theobromine is not good for you, no matter how cool the commercials are. But that doesn't stop most of us from drinking the stuff. Why? Because it tastes so good! The problem with such concoctions is that while they do take the thirst away, they only work for a short amount of time, and then you find yourself thirsty again. The Samaratin woman

Isn't it true that this is the exact same way that sin works? Sin "tastes" great, and it does work by quenching our genuine emotional thirsts, even if only momentarily. The trouble is that after we're done committing the sin, we never feel fulfilled or truly happy. We're left still "thirsty" because the sinful action we just participated in was not capable of meeting our real needs.

In John 4 Jesus meets a Samaritan woman who had fallen for Satan's slogan that sin was "the real thing," as if having sex with multiple partners was going to be able to adequately address her emotional and relational deficits and truly make her feel fulfilled and at peace. Of course, Jesus, being the architect of the heart, was and is able to see beyond the surface, to look much deeper than everyone else and zero in on the real problem:

> "Anyone who drinks this water will soon become thirsty again. But those who drink the water I give will never be thirsty again. It becomes a fresh, bubbling spring within them, giving them eternal life."
>
> "Please, sir," the woman said, "give me this water! Then I'll never be thirsty again, and I won't have to come here to get water."
>
> "Go and get your husband," Jesus told her.
>
> "I don't have a husband," the woman replied.
>
> Jesus said, "You're right! You don't have a husband—for you have had five husbands, and you aren't even married to the man you're living with now. You certainly spoke the truth!"
> (John 4:13–18 NLT)

This is a story about a lonely and troubled soul who was trying desperately to quench a spiritual and emotional thirst. There was no permanent satisfaction in the multiple relationships she had experienced. In fact, each time a relationship ended she needed to go and find a new mate, hoping that the next man would fulfill all of her emotional desires. Time and time again, however, she was left sadly disappointed. This is the reason that by the time she encountered Jesus she was into her sixth relationship. Jesus told her that she would never find the fulfillment she so desperately longed for by going to this same old well as she had been doing for years. Only he had the answer; only he had the clean, pure water that would quench these thirsts and heal the brokenness forever.

My life mirrors that woman's in many ways. Before giving my life over to Jesus, there were few things that I turned to more than homosexuality in order to quench my emotional thirsts. From my youth, with many problems in my home life and all of the fears and insecurities in my own heart, whenever I felt lonely, afraid, unloved, insignificant or unconfident, I learned to turn to homosexuality to meet those very real needs. And it worked; participating in those relationships and activities *did* leave me feeling satisfied, loved, cared for, accepted and important. After a short time, however (like the woman at the well), I was always left feeling even thirstier and more empty and alone; thereby forcing me to involve myself even further in these relationships and activities to quench the emotional thirst yet again. It was a never-ending cycle, but I just didn't realize it. The sad truth is that I spent a lot on homosexuality, a lot of time and energy just wasted; hours, days, months and even years that I will never get back. I spent a lot of money too, all on something that would never satisfy me to begin with.

God, through the prophet Isaiah, begs each of us to go to him with our needs:

> "Come, all you who are thirsty,
>   come to the waters;
> and you who have no money,
>   come, buy and eat!
> Come, buy wine and milk
>   without money and without cost.

Why spend money on what is not bread,
    and your labor on what does not satisfy?
Listen, listen to me, and eat what is good,
    and you will delight in the richest of fare.
Give ear and come to me;
    listen, that you may live.
I will make an everlasting covenant with you,
    my faithful love promised to David."
           (Isaiah 55:1–3, emphasis added)

Are we not all the same? Has not each one of us, regardless of our sexual orientation or area of brokenness and temptation, gone to the wrong well to drink; only to be left thirstier than when we began?

Terms and Conditions May Apply

This is one of Satan's greatest ploys. He loves to imitate God and sell us products promising that they will quench our emotional and spiritual thirsts. He pretends to be something that he is not. 2 Corinthians 11:14 says that "Satan himself masquerades as an angel of light." But ole Beelzebub is a fast talker in a cheap suit, with bad breath and oily hair, and you can't trust anything he says. He'll make promises galore, but it's all smoke and mirrors. His products never live up to what he guarantees, and there are always terms and conditions that he doesn't want you to pay attention to.

Have you ever noticed those commercials on the radio where at the very end someone's voice hurriedly tells you the terms and conditions so quickly you can't understand what they just said? Do you know why? They don't want you to know the terms and conditions! The seller only wants you to buy the product and ignore everything else. It's the same in the print media, too. You have to look closely, but at the bottom of many ads in newspapers or magazines you'll see this tiny print, so small that you have to get out a magnifying glass just to read it, and when you do, it's all in lawyer-speak and you can't understand what they are saying.

Satan works the same way. He tempts us to act out in any number of ways, promising that if we do we'll be happier, more fulfilled and truly satisfied. "Just do it." "There's no substitute." "Think big!" "Have it your way!" "Open happiness." "It's the real thing." The sales pitch comes in fast and often catches us off guard, and if one approach doesn't work, he's always got another angle with which to come at us. Often, the false angel of light, who is really the angel of the "bottomless pit" (Revelation 9:11 NLT), can be unrelenting as he continues begging you to sign on the dotted line. He only wants you to think of the immediate benefits, not what comes afterwards. "Don't worry about the small print," he says. "We can worry about the terms and conditions later, but first, just buy the product, do the deed, give in, and you'll feel better." *Like the Prison w/ the open door*

And if we don't stop to consider the consequences, if we can't pause even for a few seconds to contemplate what will come after, if we're unable to see the guilt, the pain, the shame, the addiction or the regret to follow, we'll give in like a chump and buy everything that the father of lies is selling. Only then will we feel the "buyer's remorse." The only trouble is, there are no refunds and no exchanges. It's purely a buy-as-is proposition. In fact, right after you've sinned, you can't even find the seller. He has skipped out of town. You're left with just this broken "product" that didn't deliver what was promised. Sin is not a very good deal after all, is it?

Don't forget, there is no such thing as a small temptation. In this regard, we should sweat the small stuff! We need to take all temptation seriously. A few seemingly insignificant temptations can quickly collide and end up having life-altering implications. It can happen really fast if you are not serious about this and if you don't deal quickly with temptations as they come. There is no need for you to suffer a spiritual blackout!

And so that's the third step of the Tempt-Away plan to defeat every temptation you face in less than sixty seconds. First, pray immediately. If you are still tempted, then escalate to Step 2: get moving! If after physically moving your body to get away from the temptation or at least distract your mind from the temptation, you are still struggling, then slow things down, pause, and take Step 3: consider the consequences. Will committing this sin really be worth it? Will it live up to what it promises? How will I feel after I do this? If you will do these three steps, and couple them with some scriptures and just plan ahead, I promise you that you will absolutely and significantly improve your ability to overcome every temptation you face in less than sixty seconds.

Step 1: Pray. 15 seconds
Step 2: Move. 15 seconds
Step 3: Consider the consequences. 15 seconds

But, Guy, what if, after doing these three steps, I'm still truly facing temptation and just can't seem to find release from its grip? What then? Turn the page for Step 4.

Small Group Discussion Questions

1. Do you agree that there are no small temptations? Why or why not?

2. Why does just saying no to sin not help us to be victorious over it in the long run?

3. Why do we so often ignore the living water that Jesus offers and go after things that leave us thirsting?

4. How can considering the consequences of our choices help us to be victorious over temptation? What are some strategies you can implement to help you overcome?

5. How different would your life look today if you had considered the consequences of choices you made in the past, and how can that impact the choices you make today? Give an example.

End Note:_____

1. Wald, Matthew. "The Blackout That Exposed the Flaws in the Grid." The New York Times. 11 Nov. 2013. http://www.nytimes.com/2013/11/11/booming/the-blackout-that-exposed-the-flaws-in-the-grid.html.

Chapter Five

The Ultimate Rope-a-Dope

Friendship...is not something you learn in school. But if you haven't learned the meaning of friendship, you really haven't learned anything.
—Muhammad Ali

Boxing used to be the most popular sport in America, but not any more. Its Heavyweight Division hasn't produced an internationally recognized star since Tyson, and the sport has relied too heavily on Pay-Per-View for revenues as opposed to making its fights available free on the major U.S. networks ABC, CBS, NBC and FOX. However, before its decline in the late 1990s, the Boxing Heavyweight Championship of the World was the richest prize in sports and the heavyweight champion was considered the world's greatest athlete.

On October 30, 1974, in a huge global event that rivaled the Olympics, the World Cup and the Super Bowl in terms of international interest and television viewership, the reigning world champion George Foreman (yeah, he's the same guy who sells the George Foreman grill on those cheesy commercials) and the former champion Muhammad Ali stood toe to toe in Kinshasa, Zaire (now the Democratic Republic of Congo). In front of 60,000 spectators who crammed into the 20th of May Stadium (the seating capacity is only 50,000) and a worldwide television audience numbering in the hundreds of millions, the two men squared off for eight and a half rounds of prize fighting that is widely considered to be the greatest boxing match in history. Ali had dubbed it The Rumble in the Jungle.

As an interesting side note, Zaire's flamboyant President Mobutu Sese Seko asked that the fight be fought in his country, eager for the attention that a huge event like this would bring, but then did not attend the match in person, watching it instead from the presidential palace for fear of possible assassination. To accommodate and maximize the primetime North American television audience, the fight was scheduled to start at 4:00 a.m. Zaire time; 10 p.m. EST in North America.

Both George Foreman and Muhammad Ali were huge celebrities, not just in the United States, but globally. Foreman was the reigning champion and considered the hardest puncher in heavyweight history. He was younger, stronger and faster than Ali and on a winning streak, having easily defeated a series of challengers in the heavyweight division. The two most serious contenders to face Foreman had been Kenny Norton and Joe Frazier, two opponents that Ali had already defeated.

As for Ali, he was a huge superstar, revered around the world and especially known for his poetic and fast tongue: "Joe Frazier is so ugly he should donate his face to the U.S. Bureau of Wildlife." "Float like a butterfly and sting like a bee." "I'm so fast that last night I turned off the light switch in my hotel room and was in bed before the room was dark." "If they can make penicillin out of moldy bread, then they can sure make something out of you." "A man who views the world the same at fifty as he did at twenty has wasted thirty years of his life." Awesome, right?

By the time the Rumble in the Jungle rolled around, however, the champ's career was in decline. In 1967 Muhammad Ali had been arrested, stripped of his Heavyweight Championship and banned from boxing because of his refusal to fight in the Vietnam War based on his religious views and moral opposition to the war. Upon his release from jail and his return to boxing in 1970, he climbed the ladder to get the opportunity to fight for the championship again, but he was thirty-two years old by 1974, considered past his prime, and much slower than he used to be.

Foreman was heavily favored to win in Zaire. Some bookmakers were in his favor 40 to 1. Gene Kilroy, Ali's business manager, when in Foreman's dressing room to watch him get his hands taped, was told by Foreman that Ali's children were about to become orphans. Foreman's trainer says, "You could smell death in the air." In fact, so concerned was Foreman about seriously injuring Ali that insiders say that just moments before the fight, the boxer and his manager actually prayed that Ali would not be killed.[1]

Behind the scenes in the challenger's locker room, handlers had secretly worried about the hospital conditions in Kinshasa and were making arrangements to transport the former champion to a hospital in Paris for medical attention if he were severely injured.

The Rumble

Although Foreman was considered the odds-on favorite by bookies, sportswriters and television sports commentators, Ali was clearly the favorite with fans in the stands that early morning. Ali entered the ring twenty minutes before George Foreman's entrance, and 60,000 people chanted in unison, "Ali boma ye!" meaning, "Ali, kill him!"

Once the fight reached the second round, Ali did something so unorthodox, so unexpected and so unconventional that it shocked the boxing world. Clarence B. Jones, a distinguished civil rights leader, colleague of Martin Luther King and friend of Ali, was at the fight sitting in row 8. Here is how he described being there that early morning:

> My initial sensation was dread. I thought this really might be Ali's last fight. I was praying and hoping he would win, but thought that if he did, it would be a miracle.
>
> Yet, as I watched Ali I had a once-in-a-lifetime view of the most extraordinary grace, elegance, and artistry in boxing. I was spellbound. I watched Ali repeatedly go to the ropes, deliberately. I began to wonder if I were witnessing some grand new boxing strategy unfolding that no one had attempted before.
>
> In the eighth round it seemed Ali was using the ropes to absorb punches, and during that process Foreman was slowing down, showing physical fatigue. The younger man seemed almost

lightheaded, as if he were boxing in slow motion. Then, all of a sudden, a flurry of punches by Ali… Foreman dropped to the canvas. He was unable to get up under the count. The referee called "knock out" and declared Ali the winner. Pandemonium broke out.[2]

Ali did something in that fight that no other fighter had ever dared to try. He held up his arms against his face and leaned back against the ropes allowing Foreman to punch away at him for eight rounds. The strongest boxer in history mercilessly beat on Ali until he could punch no more. He threw them as hard as he could, wasting all of his energy until there was nothing left. By the sixth round Foreman was exhausted and looked increasingly worn out. Ali made matters worse by taunting him saying, "Hit harder! Show me something, George" and "That don't hurt. I thought you were supposed to be bad."

Finally in the middle of the eighth round, Ali saw his moment. He bounced off those ropes and landed the final combination, a left hook that brought Foreman's head up into position so Ali could nail him with a hard right straight to the face. Foreman staggered, then twirled across half the ring before landing on his back. Foreman slowly got up but not quickly enough. The referee counted to ten and waved the fight over. George Foreman was sent into retirement and Muhammad Ali was catapulted to be the Heavyweight Champion of the World for a second time and quite possibly the greatest boxer in history, right up there with the likes of Rocky Marciano and Joe Louis.

What was Ali doing in that fight? He called his technique the rope-a-dope. Even though it looked like he was losing the fight, and losing badly, he was in control the whole time. Ali looked powerless; his corner was screaming for him to get off the ropes and fight back; fans were in shock—the great Ali looked weak. But there was method in the madness, and here was the genius of it all: Muhammad Ali took all those punches because he knew he would deliver the final blow to end the fight; he only needed to patiently wait for just the right time and then spring into action. There was design in his apparent weakness.

Jesus: The Ultimate Rope-a-Dope Champion

As you read through the Scriptures, it always appears like Jesus is on the losing side, up against the ropes. From his birth we see him poor and humble. He lived in poverty, he was ridiculed and mocked and laughed at, he lived a life of suffering, even his own family and friends doubted him, and at the end of it all, the few followers that he did have deserted him. He died owning nothing but the clothes on his back and with only one friend who returned to the cross to watch him die, John. At first appearance, one would say he lived a defeated life. But of course, we know in hindsight that this is just not true. Jesus pulled the greatest rope-a-dope of all time. Right when Satan thought he had won, right when it looked like it was all over and there was no hope, at just the right time, Jesus rose from the dead, providing forgiveness for all mankind. "You see, at just the right time, when we were still powerless, Christ died for the ungodly" (Romans 5:6). Christ's humility and giving up of control won out at the end! There was design in his apparent weakness. In this sense, Jesus' greatest strength was in his weakness.

Are You Ready for Your Own Rope-a-Dope?

Do you really want to imitate Christ's example of weakness and humility? Really? Are you open to the idea that there is divine method in this madness to appear weak? Jesus was willing to take all of those punches from Satan and all of the difficulties that life handed him because he knew he would deliver the final blow to end the fight. Are you open to this spiritual truth being lived out in your own life? Be careful, it's easy to rush to answer in the affirmative, but honestly, who likes to look weak? It is not only counter-cultural; it goes against every fiber of our being. To do so takes conviction, determination and an attitude that says "I won't concern myself with what people think of me. If folks look down on me because of my weaknesses and struggles in life, too bad; I'm much more concerned about what God thinks than what man thinks." So, I'll ask again, do you seriously desire to obey the inspired Scriptures on transparency, authenticity and openness with both God and man? I know you do; me too. But most of the time, the Scriptures are a lot easier to read and discuss and teach than they are to actually do! A lot of people want to serve God, but only as advisors. You see, if humility was the hallmark of Christ's life, and weakness was the very thing that Paul boasted about ("if I must boast, I will boast of the things that show my weakness" [2 Corinthians 11:30]), then where does that leave us?

You see, I think humility, confession and boasting about our weaknesses is the ultimate spiritual rope-a-dope. It has always been Satan's goal to shame us into silence, that we would be so afraid of what others would think about who we really are and what we are capable of that we simply could not speak the truth; and sadly, for many followers of Christ, this is their reality. Disastrously, many, many Christians have bought this lie. They are faithful to their local church fellowship that they have belonged to for years, sometimes decades. They have worshipped and served and loved and given financially, serving and giving until it hurts. They've been to more Sunday morning and midweek services than they could count and have built friendships and relationships that they cherish, yet the painful and regrettable truth is, after all of that, still no one knows who they really are. No one knows their areas of weakness and struggle. No one knows the truth about the sins they have suffered with because they have lived a life of fear and silence for so long, they don't even know there's another way.

I was raised in a home like that. My folks did all of the above many times over. They were kind and generous people who loved God and their church community, but the environment of this community was not one that encouraged transparency when it came to personal weakness, struggle and sin. I'm sure everyone must have known that everyone else was dealing with their own areas of weakness, it's just that no one felt safe enough to share it with anyone else. So mostly, people smiled and acted like all was great on Sunday, and then suffered in silence and alone. The trouble with this is that it is not God's plan for his church.

I mostly remember feeling safe and happy in my home setting as a child, but somewhere in my preteen years my mom and dad experienced great difficulties in their marriage. In spite of "who we were" on Sundays when we went to church, things were pretty screwed up behind closed doors and no one knew about it but the three of us. There were a lot of painful and hurtful things that were said and done in that house for many years. I won't get into details on who did or said what, because I love my parents, they have apologized, and I have forgiven them, but when it came to the church, that environment was not considered to be a safe place to be open and transparent about the challenges and sins that were taking place. What happened at home stayed at home, what transgressions were committed in private, stayed private. Whenever we hide sin, things *never* get better, they *only* get worse. This was certainly the case for my folks, and for me as I grew into adulthood. It is the primary reason why I have lived my Christian life with a deep conviction that I will live the opposite of how I was raised in this regard. I have been determined that I will do my best that what happens at home or in my life that is not consistent with Christlikeness, will be brought into the light with trusted, spiritual mentors who can support and advise me when necessary. My family suffered tremendously for years, all because we believed that to be honest about our temptations, sins and areas of weakness would bring disgrace and humility, when God's plan was exactly the opposite.

What a shame. Someone once said, "We can easily forgive a child who is afraid of the dark; the real tragedy of life is when men are afraid of the light." Jesus' church needs to be a place that is safe for people to be honest and real about the challenges that they face. When that is not the case and silence and secrecy are the order of the day, Satan rejoices, God weeps, and everyone suffers.

The world (and our conscience) says that we should hide our weaknesses and vulnerable parts. Yet the apostle Paul, when discussing his areas of weakness, his thorn in his flesh, tells us in 2 Corinthians 12:7b–10 a whole new way of being, one that is completely countercultural and wholly spiritual:

> *Therefore, in order to keep me from becoming conceited, I was given a thorn in my flesh, a messenger of Satan, to torment me. Three times I pleaded with the Lord to take it away from me. But he said to me, "My grace is sufficient for you, for my power is made perfect in weakness." Therefore I will boast all the more gladly about my weaknesses, so that Christ's power may rest on me. That is why, for Christ's sake, I delight in weaknesses, in insults, in hardships, in persecutions, in difficulties. For when I am weak, then I am strong.*

You Don't Have to Tell the Whole World, Just Tell Someone!

When I am invited to teach a Strength in Weakness workshop and I'm standing in front of an audience confessing to them that I used to live the life of a gay man for over a decade, a life littered with sinful and embarrassing escapades, and that I'm still homosexually attracted as a Christian, I jokingly call myself "the reluctant prophet"; but not *that* jokingly. I admit that it is still awkward to discuss so openly to so many something that would normally be so private.

That being said, it has been amazing and encouraging to me to see how affected people are by this level of transparency. Time and time again people have said, "I could never do what you're doing!" or "I could never be that open about my life!" Trust me, I get it. Speaking in front thousands of people can be terrifying enough, never mind disclosing some of the most sensitive parts of your life while doing so; and thankfully, it's not a requirement that you do this. However, I've only been involved in this kind of public ministry since 2008. For years before—in fact, since making the decision to make Jesus the Lord of my life—I was not "public," but I had as a foundational cornerstone of my faith a conviction that I must be embarrassingly transparent with at least one or two trusted spiritual friends and advisors.

The ultimate goal has been to keep these areas of temptation and weakness in the light, where they have no power over me. This has been my own personal rope-a-dope. I know that confessing homosexual temptations and attractions makes me look weak, like I'm up against the ropes, but the truth is, it is this level of transparency that gives me the strength to live a life of integrity and purity before God. That's a winner all day long in my books!

When I was living my life as a gay man, I had many secrets and told many lies in order to keep things covered and in the dark. I truly lived a double life. Living like this kept me bound and enslaved to activities and thought patterns that I knew were wrong but had no power to change. One of the methods God uses to unshackle us from habitual or even addictive sin is confession and the admission that we need help. Upon embarking on my new life as a follower of Christ, I knew that one of the keys to my long-term success would be to reverse that way of being and just tell the truth, no matter how difficult, awkward or embarrassing, and to initiate confession. And so, since my conversion to Christ that August night in 1987, I have done so. Not perfectly, of course, but before the Lord, I will tell you that it has been my habit, almost an obsession of mine, to confide my temptations and sinful misdeeds and areas of weakness and struggle to God *and* to man.

I firmly believe that had I not taken this stand and lived this way even though it's been difficult, I would be a statistic today, not a faithful Christian. My old life has come calling many times, and Satan has done his best over the years to try to lure me back; being honest about this has saved my life and my marriage.

Honesty, clarity, authenticity, trust and truthfulness versus cloaking, inaccuracy, distrust, unfairness and hiding: which of those two sound most like Jesus to you? Satan is betting that you'll choose his way; God is pleading that you won't.

Tempt-Away Step 4: Get Help!

So you're tempted, and you've kissed God by saying a quick prayer, and you've moved away from the source of the temptation and quickly grabbed your copy of *Pet Cemetery*, and you even did a fast Steve Martin shimmy; you've also considered the consequences, but you're still tempted to sin. You must now quickly move to Tempt-Away Step 4 to overcoming every temptation you face in under sixty seconds, and that is to GET HELP.

OK, good point; I get it, but Guy, how can I do that when I'm at work or on a bus or at school? If you have a cellphone or are sitting in front of a laptop or desktop, and that would include about ninety-nine percent of us ninety-nine percent of the time, you can get help fast. I'm not saying you have to have a long, drawn-out text, email or phone call explaining every detail, just a quick contact to a trusted friend or mentor that lets them know that in the next twenty-four hours, you need to speak to them for accountability's sake. It can be a text or email that is as simple as typing in "911" or "Need prayers" or "Tempted; ask me about it later." This is not necessarily the time when you need to actually speak to a person, although if you can, go for it; but life is busy and often that won't be possible. But that doesn't mean that with today's technology we can't have a prearranged person who knows that when they receive that "911" text they need to contact us as soon as they can and ask how we are and pray for us.

Text, email, phone, FaceTime, Instagram, Facebook, LinkedIn,

Google Hangouts, Twitter, Pinterest, smoke signals, whatever! In today's world, with technology as it is, there's little excuse not to reach out and touch someone (electronically speaking). Even airlines provide an Internet connection while you're 35,000 feet in the air. Let someone know you need some accountability and prayer. Just do it, no excuses. The Tempt-Away plan allows for fifteen seconds to send an email or text like that to let someone know you need help.

Here's What I'm NOT Suggesting

1. **I'm not suggesting that we have to confess every temptation and every sin we commit to another person.** How would we find the time to confess *every* sinful action committed and *every* single sinful word spoken? How would we keep track of it all? And who on earth would have the strength or desire to hear all of that? This is not about legalism and rules and fear and pressure; it's about humility before God and others, it's about not allowing Satan to have a grasp on your life where he can continually threaten you, it's about living free because we have nothing to hide. As long as we have hidden, unconfessed sin, Satan has something on us that slowly and surely will eat away at our conscience, allowing us to feel shame and suffer guilt. Transparency sets us free from all of that!

2. **I'm not suggesting that we must confess every sin even to God.** It's just not practical, and I don't see a passage of Scripture that says God even expects such a thing. Do we need to have a heart of wanting and desiring to be honest and open and real with our Father? Of course; that's what this chapter and the chapter on Step 1 (Kissing God) are all about. Does that mean, however, that we need to walk around with a pen and paper, stopping to write out every offense, keeping a detailed list so that at the end of the day we can read it to God? Living that way is administrative, authoritarian and full of pharisaism.

Besides, this would be a losing game all day long because there are times we sin and don't even know it. In Psalm 19:12–13a David differentiates between hidden faults and willful sins:

> But who can discern their own errors?
>   Forgive my hidden faults.
> Keep your servant also from willful sins;
>   may they not rule over me.

Leviticus 5:17 says, "If anyone sins and does what is forbidden in any of the Lord's commands, even though they do not know it, they are guilty and will be held responsible." So clearly our ignorance doesn't lessen the damage or take away our responsibility, but you can't confess a trespass that you didn't know you even committed. So clearly the Lord's forgiveness is not conditioned on our confession. The bottom line is, thank God that his grace and mercy and the blood of Christ are big enough to cover over every sin, whether we knew we sinned or remembered to confess it or not.

3. I'm not suggesting that we must confess our sins to people to receive forgiveness. James 5:16, the scripture to which ministers most often turn when trying to inspire transparency among their congregants, says, "Therefore confess your sins to each other and pray for each other so that you may be healed. The prayer of a righteous person is powerful and effective." Notice that James says that confession will bring about healing, not forgiveness.

4. I'm not suggesting that you must stand at a podium and publically boast about your weaknesses and sins. I am not saying that you need to make your private life everyone else's business. I appreciate the need we all have for privacy and confidentiality. I recognize that it may not be wise or beneficial or even safe sometimes to spill the beans to certain people, or even most people. They have their business to deal with; they shouldn't be worried about ours.

Let me add here for free that public confession is risky business, to be honest. Being one who lives out in the open and has spoken to tens of thousands about his weakness (being same-sex attracted) and has an international ministry devoted to this, and even authored two books on the topic, I wish to caution you that there are residual ramifications to welcoming the world into your private life, the most important of which is that everyone you are close to (parents, siblings, spouse, your children) will all have to be a part of that ride as well. It would be terribly unfair to go public with something that would affect them without explaining it to them first and even getting their permission.

So if you ever think you want to come out publically about an area of weakness or struggle in your life in the hopes that it can benefit others, either in front of an audience or online through social media, I strongly suggest that you seek much guidance from people you trust and pray over it diligently before you do anything. In other words, count the cost. It could be a life-altering decision.

Here's What I AM Saying

What I am saying is that in order to obey the Scriptures and then enjoy the numerous spiritual benefits that God has intended for us to experience via this kind of honesty and humility, you absolutely need to do this with God. You also need at least one or two trusted spiritual friends with whom you will be truly honest; somebody to whom you can tell the good, the bad, the ugly and even the nasty. Someone who has agreed to be that special person you can contact at a moment's notice via text or email when you're tempted and need some accountability later in the day, or whom you can connect with when you have sinned and are in need of bringing that deed of darkness into the light.

I Don't Have a Fixation on Confession; It Just Works

If this kind of transparency and openness has not been a regular part of your Christian life, I realize that it can be a terrifying occurrence. I get it! The fact that this has been a routine piece of my day-to-day life for almost three decades doesn't mean that it has been easy for me. It's not like I'm some kind of weird, peculiar person who has an exaggerated preoccupation or fixation on telling people my temptations, sins or problems. It goes against the grain and it is something I have had to go back and reconvince myself of several times over the years, because it is so difficult to actually live out.

In fact, if I may be so daring, I'd like to venture to say that for Christians like me who live outside of the heterosexual mainstream, it's *extra* arduous and daunting to be this open and honest with other people, more so than for those of you who are heterosexually attracted. Such a thing is hard to measure, I know, but having to confess homosexuality in a church setting is a pretty difficult thing to do, even after twenty-eight years. It has only been because of a deep, intense conviction from the Scriptures and a realistic fear of what I'm capable of without accountability, which has driven me to live consistently with this kind of authenticity with other people; so it's been anything but easy!

For the homosexually attracted Christian, in the world, apart from the church, many of us were the brunt of cruel jokes, subjected to offensive language and called mean and unkind names. We were wrongly stereotyped and considered as less than second rate. The sad truth is that even in the church, there have been times when we've had to listen to hurtful gay jokes amongst Christians who should know better, and we have often felt isolated and different from everyone else. Because of a lack of education, much of the advice and help we've received has often been embarrassingly simplistic and not very holistic in its approach. It's not easy being transparent in the church with homosexual attractions, temptations and sins, even with trusted spiritual friends.

So I understand the fear that comes from being open. Will they still love me; will they still accept me; will they gossip or slander me; will they go home and tell their wife or husband; will I lose this or that area of responsibility in the church; what will people really think of me? No one has to try to convince me of how incredibly difficult it is to be transparent, not when it is I who has had to go to other Christian brothers to humbly confess, "I just lusted after a guy that I saw on the street today" or talk about different memories of times when I acted out in my life before becoming a Christian. Believe me, I know how challenging this honesty gig is.

But God asks us to trust his plan for our lives in overcoming the bondage that Satan has tried to put us in, and a part of that plan is allowing others to help us, regardless of how difficult that may be. So if you think it's difficult to be open and transparent with your areas of weakness, imagine being in my shoes. My question to you is: are you willing to trust God in this? Even if you're not willing to trust people right now, are you willing to trust God?

Now let me tell you the real exciting part in all of this. It has been my experience that all of the fears that once inundated my heart about what others would think of me or how they would treat me were not true. They were lies that I was buying into. In fact, the opposite has occurred. I have only received love, compassion and even respect from the brothers I have turned to for accountability and help. In my twenty-eight years as a Christian, I have not once been rejected or turned away or had a friendship ruined because I humbly confessed my temptations and sins and asked for help.

Of course, I cannot promise that 100 percent of the people you talk to will respond in a godly and humble fashion, but there comes a point when you must realize that you simply can't control other people. If you run into individuals who do not understand or who are not compassionate, let that be their problem. They will have to answer to God for their un-Christlike attitude. But you too will have to answer God for how you chose to live your life. I put before you that it is God's plan that you will not walk alone in your spiritual journey, so please trust him. He will not let you down. God will help, guide and protect you as you go through this process, just as he has done for me.

How Do I Find a Spiritual Friend I Can Trust This Much?

Well, first you have to have a conviction that it's what God wants you to experience and therefore a necessary ingredient in your Christian life.

> Two are better than one,
>   because they have a good return for their labor:
> If either of them falls down,
>   one can help the other up.
> But pity anyone who falls
>   and has no one to help them up.
> Also, if two lie down together, they will keep warm.
>   But how can one keep warm alone?
> Though one may be overpowered,
>   two can defend themselves.
> A cord of three strands is not quickly broken.
>
> (Ecclesiastes 4:9–12)

Consider these two other passages on how we are to be there for each other:

> Brothers and sisters, if someone is caught in a sin, you who live by the Spirit should restore that person gently. But watch yourselves, or you also may be tempted. (Galatians 6:1)

> But encourage one another, as long as it is called "Today," so that none of you may be hardened by sin's deceitfulness. (Hebrews 3:13)

So how, practically, should you go about finding someone with whom you can be this honest? There are three criteria that you should be looking for when choosing this person in your life.

1. He or she must be a spiritually minded Christian, who is the same gender as you are and who loves God. I realize that saying that this mentor should be the same gender is a strange caveat, but trust me, you are only asking for trouble if you choose someone of the opposite sex with whom to share your personal and intimate information. The person you choose to journey with you in this must be of the same gender.

2. He or she must respect your need for privacy and confidentiality and agree that they will not divulge your personal business without your permission. The only caveat to this would be unless they legitimately fear that you could hurt yourself or someone else, which I would think is unlikely in most situations. If they ever do believe that getting further assistance or perspective from another Christian would be helpful, they must ask for your permission first before doing so.

3. He or she must be someone who will believe the very best about you when you're at your worst. It has to be someone who will believe in you when you don't believe in yourself.

If you can find a Christian who meets those three benchmarks, you've got your person. Spend a few days praying over this, asking God to give you wisdom and courage, and then if you still believe that an individual meets these three standards, ask to speak with them and tell them what you're looking for and why. If in the rare case you can't think of even one person, then pray that God will show you who they are. I would also say that while ideally it is an individual in your local home church, they don't have to be. It is ideal, but not mandatory. It's more critical that you have someone to talk to openly than it is for that person to be someone who is a member of your home church.

The Mystery of Transparency

The promised blessings of James 5:16 ("therefore confess your sins to each other and pray for each other so that you may be healed") have been proven in my life. The declaration of Proverbs

28:13 (whoever conceals their sins does not prosper, but the one who confesses and renounces them finds mercy) has equally brought peace and confidence into my heart. It is the mystery of transparency that when we humble ourselves to be honest and tell someone, including God, the truth about our weaknesses, temptations and sins, we then experience a freedom, peace and joy that cannot be found anywhere else.

Having been able to personally experience all of the benefits that vulnerability and transparency with trusted Christian friends has brought to my life, it has not only saddened me, but has deeply disturbed me how many Christians refuse to bring their weaknesses, temptations and even sins into the light.

We Need to Be Afraid of the Dark

My kids are too big to tuck into bed any longer, but when they were smaller, it was a favorite part of my day. Sometimes we'd sing a song about God; sometimes we'd talk about the day we just had and the one we were about to have; we would always say a prayer and then give one another a big hug and kiss. After this completely enjoyable ritual, my youngest son would ask me to leave a light on. He was afraid of the dark. When I was a kid I was terrified of the dark, too. At bedtime a light had to be left on, but even then, I was frightened of what lurked in my closet, under the bed or in the dark corners of the room.

In my adulthood, while I no longer need a light on to sleep, I still am leery of dark places. I don't like not seeing where I am going. I find it disorienting. I feel uneasy and unsure of myself in the dark and almost always bang into things. I don't make it a habit of going down dark alleys, and when I enter a dark room I immediately search for the light switch. When I'm brave enough to watch a horror movie, I never do so with all of the lights turned off, because that is always when the creaking starts in the other part of the house and you begin to realize that the murderer is walking around upstairs!

Not much good happens in the dark, either. Most crime is committed at night. What grows in the dark? Nothing that I would want to eat! Mold or fungi for instance, grows and even thrives in the dark. (Well, mushrooms grow in the dark...and I like mushrooms... but you get my point!)

Even spiritually, God refers to the darkness as evil. Sin loves the darkness and hates the light. In the darkness, sin thrives, grows, breathes, lives and even multiplies exponentially.

When I lived my homosexual life it didn't matter how many times I prayed and cried out to God that I could stop those sinful actions. I simply couldn't. Why? Because everything was done in the darkness, in secret, where sin loves to thrive and grow and where it saps us of spiritual strength. John 3:19–20 says, "This is the verdict: Light has come into the world, but people loved darkness instead of light because their deeds were evil. Everyone who does evil hates the light, and will not come into the light for fear that their deeds will be exposed."

It is my deepest of convictions that you simply cannot start living a free and victorious life in Jesus and break free from the hold that Satan has on you, unless you bring your dark deeds into the light. As long as you are hiding your sins and keeping them a secret, as long as you are not honest with God and at least one other Christian who can assist you, long-lasting victory over your sinful behaviors or thought patterns will never be yours.

1 John 1:5–10 (NIV1984) says:

> This is the message we have heard from him and declare to you: God is light; in him there is no darkness at all. If we claim to have fellowship with him yet walk in the darkness, we lie and do not live by the truth. But if we walk in the light, as he is in the light, we have fellowship with one another, and the blood of Jesus, his Son, purifies us from all sin.
>
> If we claim to be without sin, we deceive ourselves and the truth is not in us. If we confess our sins, he is faithful and just and will forgive us our sins and purify us from all unrighteousness. If we claim we have not sinned, we make him out to be a liar and his word has no place in our lives.

Ephesians 5:8–13 says:

> For you were once darkness, but now you are light in the Lord. Live as children of light (for the fruit of the light consists in all goodness, righteousness and truth) and find out what pleases the Lord. Have nothing to do with the fruitless deeds

of darkness, but rather expose them. For it is shameful even to mention what the disobedient do in secret. But everything exposed by the light becomes visible—and everything that is illuminated becomes a light.

Humility and How I Attained It by Guy Hammond

I like the topic of humility. I think I'm going to write my next book on it, and I'll either call it *Humility and How I Attained It* or *The Ten Most Humble Men in the World and How I Chose the Other Nine*. Actually, I suppose Christ could write those books, but he would be too humble to do so. Considering Philippians 2, of all the attributes of Jesus that simply boggle the mind, his ability to be humble tops the list.

> *In your relationships with one another, have the same mindset as Christ Jesus:*
> *Who, being in very nature God,*
> *did not consider equality with God something to be used to his own advantage;*
> *rather, he made himself nothing*
> *by taking the very nature of a servant,*
> *being made in human likeness.*
> *And being found in appearance as a man,*
> *he humbled himself*
> *by becoming obedient to death—*
> *even death on a cross!* (Philippians 2:5–8)

Of course, the wonder of this scripture is not only that Christ was this humble, but that he actually expects that those who would follow him would be this humble too!

Isaiah prophesied about him, saying:

> *He was oppressed and afflicted,*
> *yet he did not open his mouth,*
> *he was led like a lamb to the slaughter,*
> *and as a sheep before her shearers is silent,*
> *so he did not open his mouth.* (Isaiah 53:8)

Don't you see? It was this willingness to submit to weakness that gave Jesus all of his power! Forget Ali, Jesus was the inventor of the rope-a-dope.

While he walked Earth's dusty trails, he said, "Take my yoke upon you and learn from me, for I am gentle and humble in heart, and you will find rest for your souls" (Matthew 11:29). Here Jesus asks us to "learn from" him and imitate him. He often asks us to do the opposite of how the world lives. Peter says in 1 Peter 2:21 and 23:

> *To this you were called, because Christ suffered for you, leaving you an example that you should follow in his steps... When they hurled their insults at him, he did not retaliate; when he suffered, he made no threats. Instead, he entrusted himself to him who judges justly.*

The appearance of weakness was not a concern for Jesus; Christ was not interested in appearances, he was interested in reality. The reality is that he ruled the universe despite what everyone thought, and he would one day bring the world to its appointed end. So why would he care if the Pharisees or the Romans or anyone else thought of him as weak? The reality was completely different. The rope-a-dope!

Remember the scene in the Garden of Gethsemane? The guards came to arrest Jesus, armed with swords and clubs. Peter drew his sword and cut off the ear of one of them, but Jesus said to him, "Put your sword back in its place,...for all who draw the sword will die by the sword. Do you think I cannot call on my Father, and he will at once put at my disposal more than twelve legions of angels?" (Matthew 26:52–53). You see, Jesus was completely in control even though he allowed it to appear that others were in control of him. Again, Jesus' strength was in his weakness. The rope-a-dope!

Jesus is often described in the Scriptures as a small lamb. We usually think of the imagery of a small, young lamb as harmless. But there is an incredible scene in the book of Revelation. There we find the imagery of the end of times, with everyone waiting to see who would open these seals to declare judgment. Everyone was anticipating a lion, but instead, a small lamb, pure and white, came out to open the final seal, and when the seal was finally opened, "then the kings of the earth, the princes, the generals, the rich, the mighty, and everyone else, both slave and free, hid in caves and among the rocks of the mountains" (Revelation 6:15). The Lamb of God, Jesus Christ, the most humble among us, the most unassuming, turns out to be the conqueror of all the powers of the earth. The rope-a-dope!

But This Makes No Sense!

1 Corinthians 1:25 says, "For the foolishness of God is wiser than human wisdom, and the weakness of God is stronger than human strength." The bumper sticker catch phrase that "God is in control" is the reality of the situation. Jesus' humility was born out of the confidence that regardless of all appearances, he truly was the one who was in control. You can be humble when you know that you are going to win in the end. You don't have to overpower everyone and everything.

My Concern with This Chapter

Do you know what my concern is with this chapter? It is this: because the topic has been about being open, honest and transparent with other trusted Christians about our weaknesses, temptations and sins, it will be just too difficult for many to do, and they will not change. Their fear of man will overrule their trust in God. Their worry of what others will think of them or say about them will overrule what God thinks and says. The rope-a-dope analogy is cute for a chapter in a book, many will conclude, but the idea that true strength is found in weakness is just not practical in the real world. Some, I hope, will get it and change and will experience newfound freedom and peace and strength in overcoming temptation, but I wonder how many people have already stopped reading this chapter and have moved on to the next, if they're still reading the book at all.

If you still are with me, and you are still battling this idea, can I offer one more proof that this is how God intended it to be?

Can You Match the Humility of a Child?

In Matthew 18:1–4, the disciples wanted to know who was the greatest in the Kingdom of Heaven. Jesus called over a little child and told them that if they didn't change and become like this child, they would never even enter the Kingdom of Heaven. What a stunning scene! Here were all of these men, so full of themselves, so confident, so sure, so secure. I would have given anything to see the looks on their faces when Jesus asked them to step aside and make room for a small boy from the throng, taking the child into his arms and telling them that if they didn't become humble and become like this child, forget arguing about who would be the greatest, they wouldn't even get into heaven to worry about it!

We can spend our time doing many things in the name of Jesus that are no doubt amazing and impressive, but if our lives are not filled with the humility of a child, it's all a waste of time because heaven will not be open to us anyway.

What kind of qualities do we see in small children that exhibit their humility?

- Children are unashamed to show their true selves.
- They are pure.
- They are brutally honest.
- They have complete trust in their parents.
- They are eager to learn.
- Children are willing to let anyone teach them regardless of status or credentials.
- Children give and receive love unconditionally.
- Children forgive completely.
- Children don't care about prominence.
- A child is not independent, but rather dependent.

But then we grow up, and we change. We get burned and hurt and are influenced by a cold and cynical world, and we get prideful and arrogant and we lose much of that humble heart. It's almost as if we completely reverse everything we started with.

- We become afraid to show our true selves.
- We lie and deceive others to cover up the truth.
- We have a difficult time trusting people.
- We may be willing to learn, but only from those whose

credentials impress us.

- We don't give love easily, and for many, receiving love is just as difficult.

- We don't forgive as easily as we used to and often hold grudges that sometimes last for years.

- We often seek prominence, applause and plaudit and are hurt when we don't receive them.

- And we become independent. We are often too prideful to reach out for help or assistance.

And Jesus cries out to us and says, "Unless you change and become like little children, you will never enter the kingdom of heaven." Passage after passage makes it clear that humility is the way to God's heart. You can be successful without being highly intelligent, without being quick with your wit, without being clever in business or outstanding in appearance or skillful in athletics. But you cannot be successful with God without humility.

"Be completely humble" (Ephesians 4:2–3). "Do nothing out of selfish ambition or vain conceit. Rather, in humility value others above yourselves" (Philippians 2:3). "Humble yourselves before the Lord, and he will lift you up" (James 4:10). These scriptures make it clear that life as a Christian should be a daily training ground on how to be humble. It is the ultimate rope-a-dope.

So that's Tempt-Away Step 4 in being able to defeat every temptation we face in less than sixty seconds.

> **Step 1:** Pray. 15 seconds
> **Step 2:** Get moving. 15 seconds
> **Step 3:** Consider the consequences. 15 seconds
> **Step 4:** Get help. 15 seconds

OK, Guy, I completed all four steps. But what if I am still in the heat of a spiritual battle? What if I still can't seem to escape the grip that this temptation has on me. Then what?

Turn to the next chapter.

Group Discussion Questions

1. What are some of the lies Satan feeds us that keep us from being open about our sin?

2. How does confessing and bringing our sin into the light weaken the power it has over us?

3. How does openness and transparency about our weaknesses give us strength to live a life of integrity and purity before God?

4. In what ways does confession bring freedom and healing? Can you give an example from your life?

5. How is humility the ultimate rope-a-dope and how can we imitate Christ in this area?

End Notes:_____

1. Wilson, Jeremy. "How Muhammad Ali won the 'Rumble in the Jungle' with no sex, video analysis and rope-a-dope." The Daily Telegraph. 30 October, 2014. http://www.telegraph.co.uk/sport/othersports/boxing/11194851/How-Muhammad-Ali-won-the-Rumble-in-the-Jungle-with-no-sex-video-analysis-and-rope-a-dope.html.

2. Jones, Clarence B. 26 Mar. 2015. http://www.slate.com/blogs/quora/2015/03/26/rumble_in_the_jungle_what_was_it_like_to_watch_muhammad_ali_and_george_foreman.html.

Chapter Six

Lather, Rinse, Repeat

Only if you have been in the deepest valley can you ever know how magnificent it is to be on the highest mountain. —Richard M. Nixon

In 1992, American novelist Benjamin Cheever wrote his first fiction novel. It was called *The Plagiarist*. The story was about a marketing executive by the name of Arthur Prentice who became an advertising industry legend by adding just one simple word to the instructions on shampoo bottles. Adding this one word doubled sales overnight! The word was "repeat." I don't know who the real Arthur Prentice was, but whoever was the first to suggest adding the word "repeat" to the back of a shampoo bottle was a genius. What a marketing ploy! By adding those six letters to the instructions, people went through twice as much shampoo, using it up twice as fast, forcing them to rush out and buy more shampoo.

Now I'm sure that to most people the fact that this has been just a brilliant marketing ploy has been obvious for a while, but I'm not most people. Being one who believes that he must closely follow the instructions to the letter and therefore diligently reads through the step-by-step directions of any product he buys, I have been lathering, rinsing and then repeating the process since I was old enough to wash my own hair, because that's what the haircare professionals directed me to do. This has helped to ensure that my hair is as lustrous, manageable and bouncy as possible. Imagine how gullible I feel now that I have woken to the shocking truth of one of the greatest conspiracies ever perpetrated on the hair-washing public. The mysteries of Loch Ness, who killed JFK, NASA faking the moon landings, Area 51 and Elvis faking his own death are all child's play compared to what the shampoo industry successfully pulled off for the last fifty years!

All of this leads us to what I'm sure is an obvious point, but if it's good enough for *Head & Shoulders*, it's good enough for Tempt-Away. What do you do if after completing all four steps in the Tempt-Away plan, you are still in the heat of a spiritual battle? What if you can't seem to escape the grip that this temptation has on you? Then what? The answer is simply to "repeat." I mean, how can you go wrong with *more* prayer?

I'm Hardly Writing a Pauline Epistle

I realize that the methods to overcome temptation that we have discussed in this book and that I've wrapped in the branding of Tempt-Away are pretty basic. The fact that you should pray, move, consider the consequences and get help when tempted is hardly ground-breaking information for anyone who's been a Christian for longer than ten minutes. But as with most simple things in life, it's not whether you know what to do, it's whether you will do it. I'm packaging these basic tools in a format that will allow you to employ these essentials quickly and successfully.

I would also add that the *order* in which we administer these disciplines is meaningful. Many times we get moving before we pray, or we sit still to consider the consequences before we move, and most often, the idea of getting help and being transparent in the midst of temptation or even after we sometimes sin is almost completely not engaged at all. So the tools themselves, I admit, are elemental, but the application and order in which they are used as well as the speed at which we implement them have been critical aspects in my own personal success in being able to overcome temptation consistently (not perfectly).

Except in the most extreme cases when the temptation is exceptionally difficult, the allurement for sin will most often be gone by the time you've followed the first four steps as I've outlined in this book, and often, you won't even have to complete all four, meaning that usually you will overcome temptation in under sixty seconds without a problem. On the rare occasions when that is the not the case, then it's time to follow the same instructions as on the back of the shampoo bottle: repeat. Unless God is lying, which is just not possible (Hebrews 6:18), you can handle the temptation without turning to sin (1 Corinthians 10:13) and the enticement will subside (James 4:7). There are, however, extraordinary circumstances, and that is what I would like to talk about next.

For Those Facing Remarkable Circumstances

Up until this point we have been discussing the topic of temptation using the classic definition of being lured, pulled or enticed to commit a sinful act. I would like to expand the subject to consider the challenges one faces when life delivers a severe blow, some situation that is much more critical than facing a light and momentary allurement to have a lustful thought or a desire to gossip. I'm not downplaying the potential that these kinds of "everyday" temptations have to cause damage to our lives, but some people face remarkable circumstances on a day-to-day basis through no fault of their own and that most would have difficulty relating to. The kinds of temptations they must live with escalate to a whole new level the challenge to endure through difficulty.

How can one respond faithfully and patiently to the temptation to give up on one's faith, on one's self or even on life itself because the hand dealt to them is so desperately agonizing or hopeless?

Life Is Hard and Then You Die

The American science fiction author and screenwriter David Gerrold, most known for his work on the original *Star Trek* television series in the 1960s, once said, "Life is hard. Then you die. Then they throw dirt in your face. Then the worms eat you. Be grateful it happens in that order." Whether or not you appreciate Mr. Gerrold's sci-fi writing abilities, you sure can't argue with his reasoning on the difficulties of life and the end we must all face!

My kids always hated it when I threw out that "life is hard and then you die" line when they sometimes complained about how difficult and unfair life was for them because their mother or I asked them to shovel the snow, take out the garbage or empty the dishwasher. I mean, why else do you think we had kids if not to help with the chores!

I know that "life is hard and then you die" is not the most inspirational bumper sticker in the world, but I do think that once you accept its rude truth, it means you will not live in a constant state of entitlement, as if life owes you anything (a difficult concept for many). After all, the goal that God has for our lives is not that we have a problem-free existence, but rather that we know him.

As a Christian who has struggled through life with same-sex attractions since my early teens, a circumstance I did not choose and that has caused much anxiety, insecurity and loneliness for many years of my life, I know what it's like to have to be patient and steadfast in the midst of uncertainty and weakness. I know what it's like to be the brunt of people's jokes about something that is often looked down on and ridiculed. I know what it's like to live your life feeling like an oddball, different, an outsider. I know what it's like to have to deny something every day that feels so right and natural. (I'm not trying to argue against Romans 1:26–27; I didn't say it was natural, I said it *felt* natural.)

I have asked God the same question that every homosexually attracted follower of Christ has asked a thousand times: why? It has been difficult to not have the answers and somehow be satisfied and faithful in the midst of mystery and ambiguity. With this as my reality, the Christian walk has not been easy; in fact, at times it has been just plain exhausting. Overall, however, I accept this as a part of the human experience; life is hard and then you die. Why would I expect to be the only person on earth who doesn't have to suffer some kind of lifelong difficulty or challenge? Welcome to humanity!

I also realize that in spite of this lifelong struggle, my life has been charmed. I live in a country that up until now has not seen war on its soil since the early 1800s when the Canadians defeated the Americans in the war of 1812. The Canadian economy, while at times delicate and of course influenced by international markets and global events, remains stable; I am free to worship openly; I'm married to a wonderful, supportive wife and have four amazing children who can go to good schools; we live in a three-bedroom home with electricity, running water and high-speed Internet. I drive an F-150 pickup, have more than enough food to eat and my immediate family members and I have not suffered life-threatening illnesses or death as of yet. I thank God for his blessings, but I am also aware that life can turn on a dime. It did for my friend Jim.

When Life Seems Like Hell

Jim Brown is a fellow spiritual leader and counselor for a large and dynamic church in New York City, and someone who has become a good friend over the last several years. I'll never forget the first time I had the opportunity to sit with him and have a one-on-one conversation. My wife and I had just taught a parenting workshop for his congregation, and afterwards, Jim and his lovely wife took us out for lunch. While I was sure our time together would be enjoyable, I certainly wasn't anticipating that it would be life changing. What Jim shared that day and in our conversations afterwards has dramatically altered the way I think and feel about my fears and insecurities about being same-sex attracted.

In the course of conversation we were shocked to discover over burgers and fries that Jim lives with chronic pain. You would be shocked too, were you to meet him, because he is a man who is full of energy and life; he is fun loving, caring and engaging. You would never suspect that there was a time in his life when the suffering was so severe that he felt like death was the only option for relief, or that he still suffered with persistent pain. How did this gentleman go from being in such a horrific condition where he despaired of even life itself, to being the man we had sitting across the table from us, laughing, pleasant and inviting? Obviously Jim Brown had been on quite a journey and had learned somehow to manage the daily discomfort that he suffered in a wonderfully holistic manner, physically, emotionally and spiritually.

Jim's life suddenly changed forever after two successive sports injuries. The first occurred when he was forty-eight years old. He was waterskiing on Candlewood Lake in western Connecticut, in the northeastern part of the United States. A fun day out on the lake turned upside down for him when he attempted to get up on one ski. As he did, the cord tangled but then suddenly untangled, jerking his body forward and in the process, tearing his rotator cuff.

The second injury occurred two years later. Still determined to be active in spite of the previous injury, Jim went rock climbing in the Adirondack Mountains in upstate New York and suffered a complete rotator tear. After undergoing rotator cuff reattachment surgery, he was left in terrible nerve pain. Although his rotator cuff was functional, the surgery had consequentially damaged his cervical spine. He then chose to go through a painful foraminotomy where bone was cut away at both sides of the vertebrae in the hope of relieving pressure on the nerves and thereby relieving the misery. Later he had a cervical spinal fusion, but neither surgery took away the nerve pain. Something had gone horribly wrong with his cervical spine. They say "something" because it has never been determined exactly where things went awry, but it left the poor guy with severe chronic nerve pain that was almost crippling.

In a radio interview with Dr. Paul Christo, one of America's leading experts on chronic pain, Jim told Dr. Christo that "it felt like a stake had been driven through my back and left to rot, and it left me with residual pain in my arm and my chest."[1]

As well as undergoing two surgeries, Jim tried several other pain-relieving methods and a myriad of medications, all to no avail. He saw over ten doctors, trying to find any kind of relief from the suffering he was in. For almost four years, Jim's physical and spiritual health, disposition and overall well-being deteriorated dramatically. In speaking with him about this very dark period in his life, he told me how his wife and children saw him at his worst. Jim recalls how, at the depth of doing poorly, he felt like his life was being swept away. He had no strength left. Life seemed hopeless. Almost every sermon preached on Sunday mornings would leave him crying because of the severity of the pain and the sheer reality of how weak and vulnerable he had become. He told me, "Hell on earth is the place where you are hopeless because there is no chance of anything changing." He even confessed that life had become so low and the pain so relentless that he had wished to die, seeing it as the only option left to be relieved of the continual anguish he was in.

But then a miracle happened in Jim's life. Was he cured? No. Did the pain miraculously disappear? No. Amazingly, he learned methods and techniques that helped his body and his mind to be optimal, allowing him to *handle* the pain.

Jim was referred to Becky Curtis, a pain management coaching specialist who operates a clinic in Montana and also provides long-distance coaching for those with chronic pain. She is a survivor of chronic pain herself and "implemented the latest science and techniques to help her thrive in spite of excruciating 24/7 pain."[2] Jim says that when he was first introduced to the coaching program, he was "incredulous" and could not believe that coaching—primarily on how to change of his way of thinking and attitude, coupled with some other techniques—could relieve him of his suffering, but, as he says, he had tried everything else and so had nothing to lose. Jim says, "I learned pain-management strategies involving lifestyle choices and changes in the way *I think* (emphasis mine). With solutions and things I can do—instead of just suffering through the pain..." The program doesn't directly take the pain away; it helps you become optimal to be able to live with your level of pain.[3]

What did Jim learn to do differently that brought about such a dramatic change in his life? In his radio interview with Dr. Christo, Jim says that learning time management skills, relaxation techniques, how to do deep diaphragm breathing, humor therapy, diet, good sleep habits and several other approaches all combined to lower his experience of pain to a manageable level. He says that he had to constantly keep reapplying and repeating the coping techniques that his coach taught him, and within three months, he started to notice change. Within another seven months, his life and well-being had improved significantly.

Today, Jim is still in pain, but by repeating over and over again the strategies he learned, both mental and physical, the pain does not control him any longer. In fact, Jim told me that he had to finally tell his family and friends not to ask about his pain any more, because he needed to start a new chapter in his life. Most members of the church where he leads have even forgotten that he is in pain, but that is good, Jim says, because he doesn't want the focus to be on him, but on God. He reminded me of the story in John 9 and likened it to his own situation.

As he went along, he saw a man blind from birth. His disciples asked him, "Rabbi, who sinned, this man or his parents, that he was born blind?"

"Neither this man nor his parents sinned," said Jesus, "but this happened so that the works of God might be displayed in him." (John 9:1–3)

Jim Brown can't worry about the "whys" anymore, and he refuses to focus on the pain. Now being somewhat of an expert in chronic suffering, Jim says that when we have to white-knuckle our way through pain, we become narcissistic, and when that happens, we forget about all of the glory we can bring to God by living faithfully and courageously in the midst of the pain. "If you don't get your mind outside of yourself, you're limited, but when you live for God, you're living for something far greater than yourself. Your attitude then becomes 'Use me, abuse me, do whatever you wish, just let me glorify you.'"

It's important to note that this is not the kind of "miracle" that Jim had initially hoped and prayed for. That prayer was that the pain be removed. However, as is often the case, God indeed responds to our prayers, just not in a manner that we would have desired. For Jim, the miracle came in the form of learning how to strengthen and control his mind, his body and his spiritual life, which did more than reduce pain, it made him a stronger, finer and purer man for use in God's kingdom.

How Jim's Experience Changed My Life

Jim's words of wisdom and insight that day changed my life! (That was some lunch appointment, right?) Up until that day in Westchester, New York, my morning ritual had been to start my day with a quick prayer, most often before my feet hit the ground. The prayer was always the same. "Lord, thank you for raising me to a new day. Help me to deny my same-sex attractions, something that feels very normal to me, in order to be obedient to you. May I love my wife and kids and do my best to be a godly man. Amen." Then the day would begin.

I know I should have caught on much earlier, but the truth is, I had never considered the idea that I could use my homosexual attractions as something that could actually glorify God. I bemoaned my attractions to men. I had spent almost my whole life wishing they were gone. I had prayed thousands of times that I would change and become attracted to women. I felt that my homosexual feelings were only taking me further from God, so the thought that this area of my life could actually be used to glorify God was a revolutionary idea. It rocked my world that something good and wonderful and beautiful could come out of this "thing" that I had for so long hated.

So that day I decided to change my motivations. No longer would my focus be on denial, now it was going to be on glorification. Notice in my morning prayer the words "deny," "obedient," and "do my best"? My focus had been on *my* ability to sacrifice and *my* capability to obey and *my* determination to work hard throughout the day to be a godly man. There was no thought of glorifying God and displaying his power through my weakness. My approach to overcoming was using the white-knuckling and gritting-my-teeth methods to dealing with my homosexual attractions and temptations. They were narcissistic techniques, and not very inspirational ones.

Simply by changing my focus from obedience and self-denial to what Jim Brown was focusing on, which was glorifying God, while in the midst of struggle and weakness, not the elimination of it, I found new inspiration, encouragement and motivation for my life. My prayer has since changed. It is now "Lord, thank you for raising me to a new day. Help me to deny my same-sex attractions, something that feels very normal to me, in order to glorify you with my life." My day-to-day existence went from "OK, let's get through another day" to "Awesome! I get to live another day to show myself and others how amazing God is." Even though being attracted to the same gender feels "normal" to me, God will be glorified because I will refuse to let my feelings, attractions and emotions control how I will live, think and act, and whom I will follow. This attraction will not define me; Jesus will define me. Just as in Jim's case, my measure of success will not be the elimination of my struggle, but rather my ability to glorify God with my struggle. I also have learned different strategies and techniques involving lifestyle choices and changes in the way I think, with solutions and things I can do—instead of just suffering through the attractions and temptations. Living this way doesn't directly take attraction or enticement to sin away; but it does help me to become optimal in my spiritual world to be able to live successfully, and even happily with this area of weakness.

Over the years it has not been uncommon for me to hear same-sex-attracted individuals argue what I used to say to myself when I lived my life as a gay man: "I must be true to myself. I am who I am—a homosexual." For the Christian who is same-gender attracted, such an argument loses all steam when we admit that who we really are is Christians. Jesus is our identity when we decide to follow him. That reality trumps everything, including sexual orientation! Christianity is our nature and we can't truly be at peace and true to ourselves unless we are following God's path for our lives. In doing so faithfully, God is glorified.

Notice that my responsibility to deny something that feels right and natural to me has not changed, but the purpose of this self-sacrifice has transformed. Previously I rejected these appetites so that I could be obedient, whereas now I strive to refuse them in order to glorify God. Using the wise words of Jim Brown, "If you don't get your mind outside of yourself, you're limited, but when you live for God, you're living for something far greater than yourself. Your attitude then becomes 'Use me, abuse me, do whatever you wish, just let me glorify you.'"

What My Father Was Teaching Me, Though I Didn't Know It

I am reminded of one singular night in my youth. My father, who was a Christian, suffered tremendously with migraine headaches. On this particular evening the throbbing between his temples was so severe that he was forced to get out of his La-Z-Boy recliner and awkwardly crawl slowly to the middle of the living room floor to lie down. With his bedroom being up a full flight of stairs, he simply did not own the strength essential to scale them to his bed. Most of the lights in the house had already been turned off, as even the slightest beam of illumination was like a bullet through his eyes.

As I look back over those years, I literally do not recollect a day when he did not have to undergo the agonizing pounding that started just above the left eye, spread to his temples, across the top of his head and them down the base of his skull. These headaches were not the kind that could be taken away by three or four Tylenol #3s. Even more potent prescriptions like Percodan, 222s and injections of morphine; constant visits to the emergency ward (almost weekly as I grew up); acupuncture and massage therapy—whatever was prescribed and tried proved ineffective.

While the pain was almost continuous, on most days he had the strength necessary to get through his day-to-day responsibilities like one who did not have to endure such pain. But not on this night. On this night, possible relief seemed nonexistent, hopeless. There was no use in calling a cab or even an ambulance to get him to a hospital as on other evenings, since there was nothing that the medical profession had to offer that would give him release. As the tears streamed down his face, he asked me to get his Bible. I was twelve, maybe thirteen years old at the time. When I returned, my father had me sit beside him on the floor and read over and over again the only soothing words that would provide comfort for his soul. And so I began to read, "The Lord is my Shepherd, I shall not want...," the twenty-third psalm.

I didn't know what to take from this at the time, of course, but in my adult years, as I struggle with my own kind of pain, I have learned from the way my father chose to deal with his suffering, just as I have from my friend Jim's experience. When the suffering is real and life seems hopeless, when the anguish is so deep that every antidote is rendered useless, we can either become self-centered in our approach so that God gets no glory, or we can repeatedly turn to the Lord for our sustenance, and in doing so give him all the glory.

Jim Brown had to repeatedly refocus his attention on glorifying God with his weakness. He had to keep going back to learning a new way of thinking in order to take control of his life. My dad kept repeatedly going back to the Word for his strength in his times of need. How can we respond faithfully and patiently to the temptation to give up on our faith, on ourselves or even on life itself because the hand dealt to us is so desperately agonizing or hopeless? By repetitively, constantly, repeatedly focusing on using our area of weakness to continuously glorify God. Maybe the instructions on the back of the shampoo bottle were right, after all.

Small Group Discussion Questions

1. How can God be glorified through weakness and struggles?

2. What will changing your focus from obedience and self-denial to glorifying God produce in you?

3. What is it that inspires you when you hear the personal stories shared in this chapter?

4. How can the power of God be displayed in your life as you face chronic challenges?

5. What is one thing you can change that will help you in your time of weakness to find strength in God?

6. What action or thought pattern do you need to constantly repeat in order to be successful in overcoming weakness in your life?

End Notes:_____

1. Brown, Jim. "Pain Coaching." Dr. Paul Christo MD. N.d. http://www.paulchristomd.com/pain-coaching/.

2. Curtis, Becky. "Take Courage Coaching." Take Courage Coaching. N.d. http://www.takecouragecoaching.com/.

3. Brown, Jim. "What Can Coaching Do For Chronic Pain?" Take Courage Coaching. N.d. http://www.takecouragecoaching.com/what-can-coaching-do-for-chronic-pain.html.

Chapter Seven

A Bed Too Short

Be joyful in hope, patient in affliction, faithful in prayer. —Paul the Apostle in Romans 12:12

The Kingdom of Israel, before her division into North and South, had never been very good at getting along with her neighbors. To say that she had practiced little of the fine art of winning friends and influencing people since settling into Canaan would be to make an understatement. For she had, far from showing herself friendly, quite thoroughly succeeded through the years in making archenemies of virtually all the countries around her. These neighboring nations just bided their time, waiting for a chance to pounce on her and devour her, and now that Israel was hopelessly divided against herself, they had that opportunity, for the inevitable outgrowth of division is weakness.

By 722 BC, and as recorded in Isaiah chapters 28 and 29, Israel, by reason of her disunity, had rendered herself vulnerable, open to attack and susceptible to invasion. She was a sitting duck! It was only a matter of time before one or more of the surrounding bully-like nations ruled over by ambitious kings would move in to take full advantage of Israel's defenselessness. And it wasn't long in coming! Indeed, already the Northern Kingdom, the Kingdom of Ephraim, consisting of ten tribes, was in the process of being swallowed up by the Assyrian giant, whose armies swarmed over the land like locusts; and so deep was their penetration that this mighty Eastern power was threatening the borders of the Southern Kingdom as well, the Kingdom of Judah, of which the city of Jerusalem was the capital. It's at this juncture that our story opens. As we look in on the scene, as depicted for us in Isaiah chapter 28, the Assyrians draw closer and closer.

In reading the story, it's more than a little surprising to discover that the political powers in Jerusalem were not overly concerned about the prospect of impending conflict. Was their confidence based on superior military might? No. Was their confidence reliant upon their close relationship with God and his protection? No. Their reason for not being anxious about the Assyrian attack sprung from what they thought was a very clever scheme, a plan that they believed to be infallible, a conspiracy that they thought almost certainly would ensure Jerusalem's deliverance from this imminent danger from the north.

Briefly, their cockamamie game plan was this: to negotiate an alliance with Assyria, promising all sorts of attractive concessions, thinking that this would forestall the invasion and allow them the time to secretly make a counter-alliance with Egypt to the southwest. In this way, Judah could play off one ally against the other. Assyria and Egypt would then be at each other's throats, and Judah would be left alone. You'll have to admit that it was a pretty ingenious, however contemptible strategy. These "statesmen" in Jerusalem were unprincipled opportunists who sought to compensate for military weakness on the home front by making unethical moves and countermoves upon the chessboard of international politics. It was a shameful maneuver, but worse than anything else, there was no reliance on God and his ability to save them.

Not So Fast!

But wait! The voice of a prophet of God was heard in the land, denouncing the scheme as a "covenant with death," an "agreement with the realm of the dead" (Isaiah 28:18). The voice of Isaiah cried out for repentance, for reform, for honest dealing, for fair play and for dependence on God and his protection. He warned them that their plan would not work because it was the product of morally bankrupt men who acted independently of the Lord and his principles of righteousness and integrity. And what's more, he plainly informed them that it would be impossible for any plan to be successful that wasn't based upon the sure foundation of faith in God and obedience to his precepts. He told them that all of their secret treaties and plans would get them exactly nowhere and would accomplish absolutely nothing in halting the Assyrian attack, because these godless plans were inherently deficient and inadequate for the purpose. To illustrate what he meant by inadequacy, he then compared their simplistic and godless policies to that of a tall man sleeping in a short bed with a small blanket: "The bed is too short to stretch out on, the blanket too narrow to wrap around you" (Isaiah 28:20).

So, by the roundabout way of sharing that lengthy background, we've arrived at the metaphor which is serving as the basis of this chapter: a bed that is too short for a man to stretch out on and a blanket that is too small to cover him.

I'm 6 feet, 4 inches tall, with a large girth, so I've always had a challenge finding a bed big enough for me to sleep on comfortably. This predicament has only been worsened by marriage. Even though my wife and I have a king-size bed to help accommodate my bulk, it remains a challenge for me to claim my portion of both the bed and the blankets as my beautiful wife, who is obviously much smaller than I, for some unknown reason requires so much more space than I do. Also, on occasion, when I've travelled and the host has been kind enough to offer me the couch or pull-out bed to sleep on, or especially when I have been travelling in Southeast Asia where beds are not typically made for men my size, I've had to spend some pretty uncomfortable hours trying to make my 76-inch, 300-pound frame fit into a much smaller area. My feet hang over the end and there is no comfortable position for my hefty body to rest, so I know all too well what it is like to be in a bed that is too small for a man to stretch out on.

We, of course, can't know how large a man Isaiah was, but you can't help but wonder if perhaps the prophet might not have drawn from personal experience for his illustration, that there were times when he was forced to sleep in a confined area with not much of a blanket to cover himself. After all, Isaiah was married too! (Isaiah 8:1–3).

And so what is the spiritual application, you ask? It is this: that whenever we Christians leave God out of the thoughts, plans and intentions of our hearts, as these politicians did in Israel, then, like them, we create for ourselves what amounts to be a bed too short in which to spiritually stretch out. Let's go back to the historical setting in which these words were spoken. In effect, Isaiah was warning these leaders, "This thing you're intent on doing, this plot you've hatched involving Assyria and Egypt, is doomed before it begins, is bound to backfire, because it does not take God into account and is not in line with his will. Do this thing, and you will have made your own bed and you will have to lie in it, and you will find that it is too short for you, and you will not have enough covering." And so it is with us.

Two Options

What if, after doing all four Tempt-Away steps, I'm still truly facing temptation and just can't seem to find release from its grip? Then what? First, repeat the process, but next, let's discuss what you *should not* do. You should *not* come up with your own plans and schemes that have nothing to do with God, in order to defeat the enemy. When Satan comes calling, when he attacks, you always have two choices.

The first choice is to just give in to the temptation, commit the sin and attempt to make up your emotional, relational and spiritual deficits in an evil and self-gratifying manner, thus choosing to leave God completely out of the picture. Let us reason with one another: since we already know that acting out in sinful activities in order to respond to the stresses and challenges in our lives has never worked before, how is it logical that it would work now? Sin does not meet the need; it is deficient, period. It's like taking Tylenol to cure a tumor. The Tylenol might indeed mask some of the painful symptoms we are suffering, but it does absolutely nothing for the source of the pain. When the medication wears off, the pain returns stronger than ever.

I suppose you could keep taking stronger and more potent medications to dull the pain as it intensifies (indeed, it is easy to escalate our sin to keep dulling our emotional pain), but unless a surgeon removes the tumor itself, the problem will never be solved. Likewise, on the spiritual side of things, we already know that resorting to our own methods and vices to find release and satisfaction is only masking the real problem. It only dulls the pain for a short time. When the sinful action is completed, the real problem is still there. Or, as Isaiah puts it, it is akin to making a bed that is too short to lie on. As Paul says in Romans 6:21, "What benefit did you reap at that time from the things you are now ashamed of?"

The second choice you have in a time of prolonged and intensified temptation is to put your life and faith in God, trusting that he will see you through the temptation and while doing so, will also work to bring healing to the real problems in your life.

Our Problems with Option 2

There are, however, a few perceived complications with choosing God's way and not our way. First, turning to sin brings immediate gratification. Often God's path to peace and fulfillment takes longer to achieve, and we're just not patient enough to wait for that to happen.

As you are yelling at your kid in a fit of rage because of some minor incident, you might indeed be "letting off some steam" that makes you feel better in the moment. Later, though, when your teenager is hiding in his bedroom in fear because of your hysterical overreaction and the rest of your family is afraid of you because they're not sure how you will respond when trouble comes, and you're feeling guilty and ashamed for verbally abusing your child, the instant and short-lived gratification you initially experienced during the height of the assault will not seem worth it. The real issues that were bothering you that led to your instant and momentary reign of terror (fears over financial trouble, insecurity about the future, health concerns, etc.) will still be there. Or, in the words of Isaiah, your fit of rage will have been "a bed...too short."

While in the midst of it, a sexual fling with your boyfriend or girlfriend might indeed be a stimulating experience that brings immediate satisfaction. Later, however, when word gets out around school of what you've done, or what it seems you're willing to do, or when you realize that the special and loving affair could have been secretly recorded and "sexted," when your integrity is in ruins, or you come to the realization that there is a possibility of pregnancy or an STD, that tryst will not seem to have been worth it. The real and legitimate issues that led to your "need" to give yourself to someone else sexually (loneliness, insecurity, lack of self-worth, the longing to be loved, etc.) will still be there. Or, in the words of Isaiah, your premarital sexual activity with that special someone will have been "a bed...too short." (No pun intended.)

You see, acting out in some sinful manner does bring immediate release, but it is always short-lived and ultimately disappointing and maybe even dangerous. Sin is the cheapest form of satisfaction. It works, it meets the demand, but only temporarily, and while it may satisfy, it never fulfills.

It's like feeding a man who hasn't eaten in weeks a bag of Doritos for his first meal. He would no doubt feel full very quickly. In this sense the Doritos would have satisfied him and "met" the need. But we all know that within a short amount of time, he would become quite ill if the only thing that touched his stomach in a week was a bag full of Spicy Sweet Chili tortilla chips. Obviously it would have been much wiser, healthier and safer to give him something nourishing. That is what sin is like. Like feeding a starving man a bag of Doritos, it may meet the immediate demand of hunger, but it does not truly fulfill and only makes us ill a short time later. As we said in Chapter Four, the devil will have sold you a bill of goods that looked great initially but had a lot of terms and conditions secretly attached.

God knew that we would demand prompt service. Especially in today's world, we do not like to wait for anything. So the Lord pleads with us to fight against the urge to demand immediate satisfaction through sin, and to wait patiently for him in purity and righteousness:

> *You need to persevere so that when you have done the will of God, you will receive what he has promised.* (Hebrews 10:36)

> *Trust in the LORD with all your heart*
> *and lean not on your own understanding;*
> *in all your ways submit to him,*
> *and he will make your paths straight.* (Proverbs 3:5–6)

> *But as for me, I watch in hope for the LORD,*
> *I wait for God my Savior;*
> *my God will hear me.* (Micah 7:7)

Wait, Don't Medicate!

So if temptation persists, we know what you *should not* do. What *should* you do? Wait and don't medicate. I wonder how many times victory and spiritual relief has been just around the corner, but because we were not willing to be patient just a little longer, we chose sin over God and missed out on the freedom that could have been ours.

I am reminded of Daniel's situation as recorded in Daniel chapter 10. The chapter starts by showing us Daniel's deep distress over the sins of his people and their overall spiritual condition. So internally afflicted was Daniel that he had taken some friends out into the wilderness to fast and pray. They stayed out there for three full weeks. In spite of his fervent prayers for God's intercession, no response came.

Three weeks is a long time when you are distraught, begging the Lord for help. I'm sure we've all been there. It's easy, isn't it, to rush to assumptions about God when an emergency in our lives does not seem to rouse the Lord to make it an emergency for him. We can quickly start asking questions like, "Does God not care?" "Is he ignoring me?" "Am I not important to him?" "Am I being punished?" "Does God even exist?" We can't know what thoughts went through Daniel's mind by the time he reached the end of twenty-one days of prayer, but like all of us, I'm sure he was becoming a little weary of waiting. It is then, however, that Daniel, as he stood along the side of a river, received an answer in the form of a vision, and because the Holy Spirit saw fit to have it recorded, we are privileged to witness what transpired in the spiritual realm.

> *A hand touched me and set me trembling on my hands and knees. He said, "Daniel, you who are highly esteemed, consider carefully the words I am about to speak to you, and stand up, for I have now been sent to you." And when he said this to me, I stood up trembling.*
>
> *Then he continued, "Do not be afraid, Daniel. Since the first day that you set your mind to gain understanding and to humble yourself before your God, your words were heard, and I have come in response to them. But the prince of the Persian kingdom resisted me twenty-one days. Then Michael, one of the*

chief princes, came to help me, because I was detained there with the king of Persia. Now I have come to explain to you what will happen to your people in the future, for the vision concerns a time yet to come."

While he was saying this to me, I bowed with my face toward the ground and was speechless. (Daniel 10:10–15)

This passage makes it clear that God hears our prayer "since the first day" and our voices are "heard" when we pray. In this instance, dispatch in response to Daniel's supplications was sent immediately, but a spiritual battle ensued and the angel that was initially sent to help Daniel was held back and restrained for a full twenty-one days, fighting on his behalf. So severe was the spiritual battle that "Michael, one of the chief princes" had to go and fight alongside. Finally this angel was able to escape the assault and make his way to Daniel to answer his prayers.

This is an astonishing passage of Scripture that peels back the divine curtain and permits us to witness marvels much too wonderful for our physical and earthly minds to fully comprehend. All I can say is that Daniel's experience gives me hope and allows me to not so quickly be suspect of God in assuming that he is indifferent to my prayers. I'm sure there are many reasons why our appeals are not answered in the time frame or fashion in which we wish they were. Truly, God's thoughts are not our thoughts and his ways are not our ways (Isaiah 55:8).

One of the numerous reasons for the Lord's alleged silence in our time of need is that there is a spiritual battle that is raging that we simply cannot see and that, due to its intensity, the spiritual reinforcements just can't reach us right away. Does not Hebrews 1:14 say, "Are not all angels ministering spirits sent to serve those who will inherit salvation?" How sad it would be to discover that we abandoned the fight and gave in to temptation unnecessarily and too early simply because we were not willing to wait for the angels who were indeed dispatched, but because of this spiritual skirmish, just weren't able to reach us in a time frame we thought they should.

So when temptation arrives, and we've prayed and moved and considered the consequences and sought help from a friend, is it not too much for God to ask that we just calm down, chill out and control ourselves while we wait for his response, rather than self-medicate? Scriptures even promise that if we will just hold on and resist the devil, he will flee and relief will arrive: "Submit yourselves, then, to God. Resist the devil, and he will flee from you" (James 4:7).

The Still, Small Voice of God

Christ would not be born for another 906 years. Elijah, the prophet of God, having incited the wrath of the wicked Queen Jezebel, had been compelled to flee for his life into the desert. After three days of running and with some ninety-five miles behind him, Elijah arrived at a tiny town where he left behind his attendant who had been traveling with him, while he trudged on alone another whole day's journey further into Judah's wasteland. He kept moving forward until his body was utterly fatigued. Finally, he decided to stop and found shade from the scorching desert sun beneath a tree.

And here, in the shade of the old tree, his soul no less exhausted than his body and his heart heavy with dejection, frustration and discouragement, he prayed a pitiful prayer: "'I have had enough, Lord,' he said. 'Take my life; I am no better than my ancestors'" (1 Kings 19:1–5). In other words, "I've had it. It's over. I can't go on any more. Kill me now."

And with that, Elijah promptly fell into a deep sleep, a sleep from which no doubt he hoped he would never wake up. But it was not yet time for him to die. God had other ideas. He sent one of his angels to wake the prophet out of his sound sleep, and the angel commanded him to eat a supernaturally provided meal. No preparation or drive-thru necessary; God provided the meal (not a good time to complain about the cooking!). And when Elijah had his fill, he lay down and fell asleep again, only to be awakened by the angel a second time and made to eat another meal.

Finally rested and having regained some strength, Elijah was able to push on for approximately another ninety miles in a northeasterly direction until at long, long last he arrived at his destination, the base of the mountain of God, Mount Horeb. This mountain was the holy mountain of Exodus, referred to as the "mountain of God" in Exodus 3:1. Here the Lord told Elijah to climb to the top of the mountain and stand there and wait, for the majesty of God was about to pass by.

God Speaks

When Elijah got to the summit, a mighty wind of hurricane force abruptly arose. The power was so magnificent and mighty that huge boulders were split in two by the strength and sound of it. Elijah looked for God to appear in the mighty wind, but God was not in the wind. Soon after, a gigantic earthquake occurred so that the whole mountain shook with the force of it. Elijah looked for God to appear in the earthquake, but God was not there. Soon after, a blazing fire roared through. The mountain itself seemed to belch crackling flames. Elijah, desperate to hear from God, looked, but God did not appear in the fire. On the heels of these natural and yet unnatural phenomena, there followed a few moments of absolute quietness, the silence of which was deafening. And it was there, out of the eerie soundlessness, that a gentle whisper was heard. It was the whispering voice of God himself: "What are you doing here, Elijah?" (1 Kings 19:13). In other words, "Why did you run; why were you so afraid?"

This is such a fascinating and beautiful story. The New American Standard Bible says that the voice of God was "a sound of a gentle blowing." The King James Version says it was a "still small voice." Moffatt, in his translation of the Bible, says that a "breath of a light whisper" was audible. Think of it. God's voice was so gentle, so light, so caressing, that Elijah could barely hear it. God tickled Elijah's ear with the breath of his mouth when he uttered to him his will, which was not at all what one would have expected from God if he were to speak to any of us audibly.

We would rather that God would reveal himself in some spectacular manner, like out of a hurricane, earthquake or fire. Instead, however, it best suites his divine purpose to talk to his children with a minimum of display and sound. This is the "still small voice" of God. That expression is loaded with suggestion!

For instance, consider God's nearness. Whispering is a unique form of communication. It implies that the message spoken is so special that it is for your ears only. Someone doesn't whisper from across a room, one whispers only when he or she is near and extremely and intimately close to someone else's ear. In fact, for me, other than my wife or children, for someone to whisper that gently into my ear is uncomfortable. So if God speaks to us at times in a "still small voice" today, it is a good indication of his closeness. When God whispers to us, it is proof enough of his nearness to us.

Today, I would think it highly unlikely (not impossible, just not probable) that one would actually audibly hear the voice of God. I won't argue with someone who says they've heard it; I'm just saying such an occurrence would be extremely rare and certainly I've never had the privilege. That being said, God still speaks to us in a "still small voice" through his word, through the Holy Spirit and during times of quiet meditation and silent reflection in prayer.

God tells us in Psalm 46:10 (NLV), "Be quiet and know that I am God." But how do we hear the still small voice, the whisper of God above all of the noise and racket of our lives? We don't live lives that are very quiet. With smartphones and Facebook, with television and Xbox and PlayStation 1, 2, 3 and 4, movies, DVDs and Blu-ray—the list goes on and on—it's hard to listen to God. It's almost like his voice must come in the form of an earthquake or hurricane because that would be the only way he could get our attention!

It helps me, in the time of temptation, when I am waiting for the tempter to flee, to calm my mind, turn the volume of the world down and try to listen to God. Turn off the television. Shut the computer off. Put down the controller. Shut off the smartphone. What? I know; it's not easy, but you won't die; all of your friends and the world will still be there when you go back to it all. Be still and listen for the still small voice of God. If you can't hear him, it's not because he's not speaking; it's because life has become too loud and busy, and we can't hear him anymore.

Your Hidden Life

While this holy battle rages and we are left patiently waiting for the temptation to depart, there is an important element of the Christian life that should offer us great comfort and security as we wait. We find this spiritual truth in Colossians 3:3. It's just a little line that often is overlooked, but what an amazing statement it is!

> Since, then, you have been raised with Christ, set your hearts on things above, where Christ is, seated at the right hand of God. Set your minds on things above, not on earthly things. **For you died, and your life is now hidden with Christ in God.**
> (Colossians 3:1–3, emphasis added)

The Bible teaches that when we turn ourselves over to Christ, our old life dies and we are raised with Christ. When a person was dead and buried, the Greeks very commonly spoke of him or her as being "hidden in the earth"; but the Christian has died a spiritual death, and is not hidden in the earth, but in Christ. What a beautiful thought.

Why do people hide things? If you were to come into my home, you would discover that things often get hidden. Every now and then, we will come across a gift that was meant for last Christmas, but we had hidden it so well from the kids that when Christmas came, we couldn't find it! Then in May or June, during spring cleaning, all of a sudden it pops up. Candy is often found in mysterious places, as everyone tries to hide their own private little stash away from everyone else. I'm sure all of us have a bank account where we hide our money to ensure that it is safe. Others have safety deposit boxes where the things they own are so treasured or so secret that they must be kept in a vault behind lock and key.

Then of course we know that some have gone to extraordinary lengths to hide things from others. So expensive, so treasured, is the item that they bury it. In Nova Scotia, on Canada's Atlantic coast, there is an island not too far from where I once lived called Oak Island, where there is a treasure pit. It is almost 200 feet deep, and it is protected by an elaborate set of booby traps or underground channels to the ocean beach over 500 feet away. It has been the subject of countless excavations since 1795, costing millions upon millions of dollars, and has been the death place of six treasure hunters who have given up their lives just to see what's down there. It's remarkable that with today's technology, no one has yet discovered what is at the bottom of this 200-foot tomb, but as of the writing of this book, we still don't know. What *is* down there? What could be so precious as to be buried so elaborately?

The most popular theory is that it is a treasure of the eighteenth-century pirate Captain Kidd, who frequently visited the region of Oak Island to rest and repair his ships. He seemed to have a habit of burying the treasures he plundered far and wide. Then there is the even stranger theory, that the crown jewels of France are buried there. They went missing in 1791 and are said to have been taken to Nova Scotia by the French. When the British attacked, the French supposedly buried them on Oak Island to keep them safe. Whatever is down there, it is so spectacularly valuable that someone went to extraordinary lengths to hide it and to ensure that no one can get to it, steal it or damage it.

This is what Christ has done with us. We know that when we give our lives to Christ, three things occur: 1) our sins are forgiven, 2) the Holy Spirit comes to live inside us and 3) we are added to God's church. As Deuteronomy 14:2 says, "For you are a people holy to the Lord your God. Out of all the peoples on the face of the earth, the Lord has chosen you to be his treasured possession."

So precious is the Christian that God has hidden us, like the treasure on Oak Island. God went to extraordinary lengths to bury us so far away that no one in the spiritual realm could get to us. Likewise, with Jesus, you and I are protected from the devil, sheltered from the storms of life, and completely covered with the mercy of God by the blood of Christ.

Paul's words in Colossians 3 are wonderful. He says in effect that, just as Jesus Christ died and subsequently rose from the dead (only to disappear from the sight of men at his ascension back to heaven, and there to remain visually hidden from the sight of man until his second coming), so we Christians, because we died to sin at our baptism and rose to a gloriously new life, have also been hidden "with Christ in God." In the spiritual realm we are tucked away in a special place, because God's children are so valuable to him that he wants to ensure that nothing happens to us until the appointed day, so he hides us with Christ. The Christian life is the hidden life.

In Psalm 83 David boasted that the Israelites were the "hidden ones" of God (KJV), and because of this special relationship as God's chosen people, they were safe and secure from all alarms. We Christians are today the "spiritual Israel"; we are his chosen ones in the protective custody of God, no less than were those Hebrews of yesterday.

It's like we are in God's "witness protection plan," much like what police forces do when they have a special witness that must be protected. That person is given a new name, a new identity, a new job and a new home, and hopefully is so well hidden away and concealed that those who want to find him or her couldn't, no matter how hard they tried.

In fact, as God's chosen people today, we are even *more* hidden than the Israelites were as God's chosen people of yesterday, because while they were hidden in God, we are hidden *with Christ* in God. We in effect get the "double whammy" of protection. Isn't it incredible and amazing to know that you are a person who is tenderly wrapped and safely concealed in the arms of Jesus? And no harm can come to the one who is safely concealed in the arms of Jesus. Talk about eternal security!

When we are in the midst of temptation and challenge, when it appears that God is not paying attention to our prayers, we can ask questions like: "How secure is my forgiveness? How locked away is my salvation? Maybe heaven is for everyone else, but I, no doubt, am going to blow it here so that I won't make it. Where is God when I need him?"

Well, let me put it to you this way: according to the scriptures we have read, if you ever fall from the grace of God, it will not be for the reason that God's hold on you was insecure; rather, it will be that your hold on God became insecure. It will be because *you left him*, not because he left you. But so long as you choose to remain in the everlasting arms of God, hidden with Christ, secure, then Satan may throw his arrows at you, he may indeed strive to get you to loosen your grasp and even leave God, but the protective shield of God's love will save, preserve and protect you, because *your life is hidden with Christ in God.*

The Living Stones of God

Did you know that inside the temple that Solomon built, not a single stone was visible? The stones were completely hidden beneath a covering of red cedar wood, which was an emblem of atonement.

> *So Solomon built the temple and completed it. He lined its interior walls with cedar boards, paneling them from the floor of the temple to the ceiling, and covered the floor of the temple with planks of juniper. He partitioned off twenty cubits at the rear of the temple with cedar boards from floor to ceiling to form within the temple an inner sanctuary, the Most Holy Place. The main hall in front of this room was forty cubits long. The inside of the temple was cedar, carved with gourds and*

open flowers. Everything was cedar; no stone was to be seen.
(1 Kings 6:14–18)

In the same way we Christians, as living stones, combine together to build a spiritual temple. Look at what the Scriptures say in 1 Peter 2:4–5:

As you come to him, the living Stone—rejected by men but chosen by God and precious to him—you also, like living stones, are being built into a spiritual house to be a holy priesthood, offering spiritual sacrifices acceptable to God through Jesus Christ.

What does that mean for you and me? It means that each of us today is a stone, a living stone. We have been quarried out of God's great quarry, the same one that Abraham and Sarah and Moses, Isaac and David and Ruth, Peter and John came from! God has been working in us with his great hammer, shaping us into exactly who he wants us to be so that we can fit into his church in the exact place he has set for us, as painful as that process may often be.

This is why we are told:

Consider it pure joy, my brothers and sisters, whenever you face trials of many kinds, because you know that the testing of your faith produces perseverance. Let perseverance finish its work so that you may be mature and complete, not lacking anything. (James 1:2–4)

With every trial, with every test of our faith, with every challenge and with every temptation, God, the great architect of the heart, is molding us and making us into "living stones" with which are built a tremendous temple in which the spirit of God lives.

God in effect says, "I have a place designed for you, and you belong exactly where I want you to be." And each stone is carefully and thoughtfully placed in the temple of God, his church. And then, just as Solomon was told to hide every stone with cedar, to cover over every stone of the temple of God with beautiful paneling, we too, as living stones, are covered with his atonement. We are blanketed in grace. We are hidden in mercy. You are totally and completely covered in atonement, because God considers you to be so precious, so expensive and such a treasure that you have been hidden with Christ in God; the safest and most hidden spot in the universe, both physically and spiritually.

So take heart. Do not be down. Do not let yourself think that your prayers are unheard or that God is uncaring about the struggles you are facing; it's not true. You're too special, too treasured, too expensive and too hidden by the Lord.

As Isaiah cried out to the statesmen and leaders of Jerusalem as the Assyrians drew near, so he cries out to us that to turn to our own plans and schemes, to our own devices, to get our legitimate emotional, relational and spiritual deficits filled is a waste of time, a bed that is just too short for us to spiritually stretch out on.

Small Group Discussion Questions

1. Can you think of any difficult circumstances in your life when you relied on your own wisdom and plans, and not God's? How would things have gone better had you done it God's way?

2. Comment on the example of sin being akin to feeding a starving man a bag of chips. How is sin the "cheapest" form of finding satisfaction and fulfillment?

3. Why are we often not willing to wait for God's answer in our lives?

4. What are your thoughts about the story of the angel having to fight for twenty-one days before Daniel's prayer could be answered? Do you think this still happens today?

5. How do you feel about being "hidden with Christ in God"? How will this change how you think and act?

Chapter Eight

It's All in How You Bounce

I never thought of losing, but now that it's happened, the only thing is to do it right.
—Muhammad Ali

On Monday, November 1, 2010, Doctor Philippe Bensignor and his son were having a drink in a local café in their north end Paris neighbourhood when suddenly something astounding occurred. The doctor's son noticed that at an apartment building across the street a baby who had somehow crawled through the railing of a seventh floor balcony was creeping dangerously close to the edge and surely about to fall. The two raced across the street just as the 18-month-old infant boy plunged to what was his certain death. Miraculously, the child landed on the awning of the café below which served as a trampoline, bouncing the child up into the air and right into the arms of Dr. Bensignor who had arrived just in time before the child could hit the pavement. The stunned doctor looked the baby over and found no injuries. The baby had fallen sixty feet and barely had a scratch!

"At that moment you don't have time to think; I just had enough time to check I was in the right position," said the doctor.[1] As if this story couldn't be more remarkable, at that time of the evening, the canopy that the baby fell on normally would have been folded away but was not because the mechanism had broken the day before, leaving it open for the baby to fall on. The doctor said he was "standing at the right place, at the right time."[2] I'll say!

As incredible as this story is, the truth is that it's not all that unique! There are numerous news reports of young children falling from unbelievable heights and enduring falls that adults could never survive. "Children are more resilient," says Dr. Alistair Sutcliffe, senior lecturer in pediatrics at University College London. "It's simple physics. They have chubbier bodies and a higher proportion of body water so they are more robust to injury. They have more padding around their bodies and they generally recover quickly."[3]

Commenting on a tot who survived an incredible fourteen-story fall in Minnesota in 2014, Tina Slusher from the pediatric intensive care unit at Hennepin County Medical Center said "If you and I fell that far, we'd be dead" but "He's a baby and...they tend to be more flexible and pliable than you and I would be."[4] That tyke in Minnesota had suffered serious injury, but survived nonetheless and made a full recovery! This puts a whole new spin on the term "bouncing baby boy," doesn't it?

What's my point? It is simply this. We are all going to suffer spiritual falls. Hopefully most of the falls will be more like stumbles or tumbles, but I would think it true that for every Christian, there will be a time in your life when the fall is really more like a plunge or nosedive. The question is not whether or not this could happen to you, the question is, when it does, will you "bounce" and survive, or will you just suffer a cataclysmic crash that guarantees spiritual death?

As Muhammad Ali once said, "I never thought of losing, but now that it's happened, the only thing is to do it right." I appreciate the ex-champ's sentiments, and while it's possible to box your way to the heavyweight championship of the world and not lose while on that journey to the top, that is certainly not the case in the spiritual ring. In fact, we will all sin practically every day in some way. As it says in Romans 3:10–12:

> "There is no one righteous, not even one;
>   there is no one who understands;
>   there is no one who seeks God.

All have turned away,
>   they have together become worthless;
there is no one who does good,
>   not even one."

And as if we needed any further convincing, Isaiah 64:6 says, "All of us have become like one who is unclean, and all our righteous acts are like filthy rags."

This brings us full circle back to the first chapter of this book where we discussed the importance of knowing how to fail well. The hard truth that we cannot live a perfect life as a Christian does not sit well with many who call themselves Christian. I speak to these unrealistic souls all the time. Our churches are full of them. They beat themselves up and bemoan their inability to live life flawlessly. "I just don't do well with failure," they'll say. Well, without wanting to offend too severely, may I say this? Get over yourself! Not only is it impossible to live a sinless life, as I pointed out in the first chapter, it's not even God's expectation or plan that you do so, and for you to moan and grumble over your daily imperfection is an insult to God's blueprint for your life. If you don't sin, then there is no weakness, nothing to boast about, nothing to glorify God with and nothing to stay strong for.

The reality is that we all know we're sinners; it's just that many of us are too full of pride and arrogance to let our weaknesses show to anyone else. This is why it drives me nuts when I see followers of Christ strive to look so perfect and well put together. This sinful attitude almost always accompanies having a judgmental heart against others who are struggling through their Christian life with weakness and sin and doing so in an honest and humble manner.

Listen, we're all broken. There is no one who needs the blood of Christ more or less than anyone else, regardless of your area of weakness and temptation. So we will all fall repeatedly. The only question is, how far will the drop be, and will we survive it? That is one of the purposes of this book, not only to assist you in attacking and quickly overcoming the daily temptations that we all face, but also to learn how to minimize the damage when we do sin.

In the introduction, here is what I promised you would get by reading through the book:

I promise you, if you faithfully and consistently follow the four-step protocol that I offer in this book whenever you are tempted to sin, regardless of the type of temptation you face, you will find that the number of times you give in when enticed to sin will drop dramatically and your levels of personal righteousness will skyrocket to new heights. This program will work no matter where you are in your spiritual journey right now, whether you've been a Christian for thirty minutes or thirty years, whether you have the role of elder, pastor or evangelist or can barely find your way to church on Sunday mornings.

To top all that, this book will explain this four-point game plan, my reasoning behind it and the biblical teachings to back it all up, along with some great tips to help you be successful. You will find that in real time you are able to actually implement as many of the four steps that you need to in order to overcome temptation, most often within thirty to sixty seconds, meaning that this is a method you can successfully put into practice as many times as you need to, all through the day and night, no matter where you are or what you are doing.

So, perfection is not the goal, but faithfulness is. As the Christian author Henri Nouwen so rightly said, "What you choose to do with failure is perhaps the most profound indicator of who you are and who you will become" as a Christian.[5] If you don't know how to fail well as a follower of Christ in the short term, it will dramatically decrease the chances that you'll even stay a Christian in the long term. Sadly, there are too many people who have unnecessarily become a statistic, representing the number of those who have quit the faith, all because they couldn't handle failure. In other words, they didn't bounce.

Why Strive for Something You Already Own?

Besides, why do we tire ourselves in the pursuit of something we already own? In the spiritual realm, God has already made the Christian perfect, completely righteous (Romans 4:23-25; 2 Corinthians 5:21). You and I don't need to try to be righteous, we already are! We certainly do have a responsibility to live lives of integrity before God ("shall we go on sinning so that grace may increase? By no means!" Romans 6:1–2), but in an altogether paradoxical and perplexing manner that only God could contrive, and one that simply boggles the mind, he has made it possible for fallen man to be perfect, that is, to come into contact with the blood of Christ, which will cover over every sin we have ever committed or ever will commit, provided we stay faithful (not perfect, but faithful) to him (Ephesians 2:8; 2 Corinthians 5:17). The inexplicable part of this is that the only way to get this gift is to actually sin. Is that crazy, or what? Our weaknesses are actually our only road to God. If you're not a sinner, then you don't need Jesus!

The ultimate goal of our earthly existence should be to have a loving, meaningful, personal relationship with the Lord and to glorify him with our lives (1 Peter 2:9; Ephesians 1:11–12). Our desire to do our best and not sin should never come from some place that desires perfection for perfection's sake. You could spend your whole life attempting not to sin, following a list of rules and laws, and it could have nothing to do with loving God. Wasn't that the problem that Jesus had with the Pharisees and religious leaders of his day?

The Bible was never meant to be some sort of behavior modification course; it's a love story about a Father who so desperately adored his children that he was eager to sacrifice his life for theirs. Although behavior modification is not the goal, a dramatic change in our behavior should naturally follow as a response to that kind of love. Titus tells us as much in chapter 2 verses 11 and 12:

> For the grace of God has appeared that offers salvation to all people. It teaches us to say "No" to ungodliness and worldly passions, and to live self-controlled, upright and godly lives in this present age.

The inescapable reality that we will sin does not take away our responsibility to try our best; it is up to us to keep moving forward, to try to improve and do better, to progress closer and closer to Christlikeness, which is perfection. Just because perfection is unattainable doesn't mean we don't endeavor to improve.

Every athlete knows that they will suffer injury, make mistakes, go out of bounds, miss the pass, hit the post, fall off the beam, miss the uprights, drop the ball, strike out, get a yellow card, commit a personal foul, and on a really, really bad day, even score on their own goal, and we're talking about professionals who are paid millions because they are the best of the best in their own sport. An athlete knows they'll never be perfect, but that reality doesn't allow them to quit. No, they love their sport too much for that, so they strive, they practice tirelessly, they examine their own play to look for weaknesses and mistakes so they can learn from them and improve and do better. In this Christian experience, we are to strive on and not quit, because we love Jesus too much to do that. We understand that while we will fail, we will learn from these difficulties and continue to go all out.

Notice the forward progression of the faith of a follower of Christ: we are "being transformed into his image with ever-increasing glory" (2 Corinthians 3:18). Paul labored with the Galatians, he said, "until Christ is formed in you" (Galatians 4:19), and he told the Christians in Ephesus that their goal was to attain "to the whole measure of the fullness of Christ" (Ephesians 4:13). Perfection in the physical world is not possible, but we strive to move forward faithfully, becoming more and more like Jesus each day, and while we do so we celebrate that perfection is our reality in the spiritual domain.

3 Steps to Failing Well

As Ali said after failing, "the only thing is to do it right." Yes, there is a right way and a wrong way to fail in the Christian life. As one who has failed many times but keeps bouncing back up again, here are the important ingredients to failing well that I suggest you implement.

1. **Realize that you can always pull out of a spiritual nosedive.** Imagine you are on a flight to sunny Honolulu, Hawaii for your next vacation. "Yeah, right," you say. "I can barely afford a 'stay-cation' much less spend a few weeks on Oahu." I know; that is why I asked you to imagine. Stay with me. So you're on this flight and just like in the movies, it turns out that your pilot and copilot are actually international villains on the run from the FBI and Interpol. To escape with the stolen money and jewels, the two of them just grabbed their parachutes and jumped out of the plane, which is now starting to nosedive (so I've got a healthy imagination; at least my therapist says it's healthy). As the other passengers panic, you rush to the cockpit to save everyone on board (good career move).

Once in the pilot's seat, you can see that the gauges in front of you are whirling out of control, showing your rapid descent as the aircraft plummets to the ocean below. You know you need to act quickly because the faster the plane falls from the sky, the more difficult it will be to pull up and out of the nosedive. What should you do? Well, I don't know; I'm not a pilot and have obviously never flown a plane before. What are you asking me for? That being said, after watching a lot of movies where this situation has occurred many times, I would suggest you grab the control wheel in front of you (called a yoke in pilot-speak) and pull it back as hard as you can to pull the plane out of the nosedive. Of course, after you do this, you'll still need to figure out how to land the jet, but that's not my problem. Anyway, the point is, when the plane is in a nosedive, you wouldn't think, "Oh well, I guess we're going to crash" and then do nothing. No, if you were able, you would do all you could to save the plane from crashing.

In our Christian lives, if we're not careful, we can start to nosedive spiritually when we don't repent immediately and one sin piles on top of another. It can be easy to think after a while that it's too late to repent, that we've gone too far and there is no way back. The Satan loves this, and in fact, it is his goal. He doesn't just want to get you to sin; he wants you to crash your life to the bottom of the ocean. The good news is that in Christ, you can always pull out of the nosedive. There is never a need to think, "I've gone too far, I've sinned too much, there is no hope, so I might as well just go all the way and crash." 1 John 1:8–2:2 offers the lifesaving technique to pull out of the spiritual plummet:

> *If we claim to be without sin, we deceive ourselves and the truth is not in us. If we confess our sins, he is faithful and just and will forgive us our sins and purify us from all unrighteousness. If we claim we have not sinned, we make him out to be a liar and his word is not in us.*
>
> *My dear children, I write this to you so that you will not sin. But if anybody does sin, we have an advocate with the Father—Jesus Christ, the Righteous One. He is the atoning sacrifice for our sins, and not only for ours but also for the sins of the whole world.*

Isn't that amazing?

There were times in my Christian walk, especially in the first decade, when I would often become so discouraged after sinning in some manner that I would take hours, and sometimes even days, to recover spiritually. I would feel guilty and distant from God and think, "Why would God want to hear from me?" If this has been your habit, listen to me. A bad few minutes does not need to become an hour. A bad morning doesn't need to become a bad afternoon. A bad day doesn't need to turn into a bad week. And, Lord forbid, if you have a bad week, it certainly doesn't need to turn into a bad month or a bad year! You can always pull out of the nosedive. Catch your breath as you read these scriptures:

> For his anger lasts only a moment,
> > but his favor lasts a lifetime;
> weeping may stay for the night,
> > but rejoicing comes in the morning. (Psalm 30:5)

> Call on me when you are in trouble,
> > and I will rescue you. (Psalm 50:15 NLT)

> I have swept away your offenses like a cloud,
> > your sins like the morning mist.
> Return to me,
> > for I have redeemed you. (Isaiah 44:22)

> Once you were alienated from God and were enemies in your minds because of your evil behavior. But now he has reconciled you by Christ's physical body through death to present you holy in his sight, without blemish and free from accusation. (Colossians 1:21)

> My power is strongest when you are weak. (2 Corinthians 12:9 NIRV)

2. Return to God immediately. I have four children. My oldest daughter, who is now in her twenties, has always loved the way I smell. I know this might be surprising to those of you who know me, because you may have been near me when I might have offered an aroma that you didn't appreciate. But in spite of these rare occurrences, ever since my daughter was very young, she has always liked my natural "aroma." When she was in her preteen years, she often tried to wear my shirts and T-shirts around the house because she said they smelled good and reminded her of me. I used to have this big lumber jacket that I liked to wear, that is if I could get it off my teenage daughter. You see, by doing this, she could feel close to me, even when I was not present. I submit to you that this is the way we should feel about our spiritual Father, just wanting to be near him all the time. In other words, we need to love the way God smells.

The one thing, however, that will cause there to be distance between us and the Lord is our sin. The question is, how long do we want to feel that separation from God? That time frame is entirely in our own hands. You can return immediately, or you can return days later after you've wallowed in self-pity; the choice is completely up to you.

Isaiah 57:15 says:

For this is what the high and exalted One says—
he who lives forever, whose name is holy:
"I live in a high and holy place,
but also with the one who is contrite and lowly in spirit,
to revive the spirit of the lowly
and to revive the heart of the contrite."

One of the secrets to failing well is to not allow there to be any space between the time you sinned and the time you are praying. As soon as you recognize that you have sinned, pray.

The classic example of having this kind of attitude is the story of Zacchaeus in Luke 19. As a tax collector on behalf of the Romans, the little guy was a real snake of a man. Zacchaeus would charge extra tax to people who were poor and already paying too much so that he could keep the extra for himself. He was a notorious extortionist. But when Jesus ate with him, Zacchaeus underwent a change of heart. In declaring that he would stop stealing from his neighbors and make restitution, he taught us what real repentance looks like. He had a here-and-now attitude. All too often we feel like we need a cooling-down time before we can pray. "I'm too mad right now." "I'm too hurt." "I'm much too angry." "I need time to repent." When Zacchaeus decided to repent, he did it "here and now" with no hesitation.

The real exciting news is that revival always follows repentance. Don't hesitate in your return to the Lord. If you want to bounce and not crash after sinning, then pray immediately after you've transgressed. Do it now. Do it quickly. Love the way God smells.

3. Be merciful with yourself. Jesus says in Matthew 9:13, "But go and learn what this means: 'I desire mercy, not sacrifice.' For I have not come to call the righteous, but sinners." Most Christians are big on sacrifice. We sacrifice our time, we sacrifice our energies, we sacrifice our sleep, we sacrifice our money, we sacrifice our emotions, all in the name of Christ. But sacrifice is not the thing that pleases Jesus. Why? It's not because sacrifice is not essential, because the truth is, sacrifice is an important tenet of the Christian faith. I think sacrifice does not please Christ because it can be our tendency to sacrifice, to give or to work hard out of a heart of legalism, as opposed to doing so out of a heart of love. Indeed, Paul says this very thing in 1 Corinthians 13:

> If I speak in the tongues of men or of angels, but do not have love, I am only a resounding gong or a clanging cymbal. If I have the gift of prophecy and can fathom all mysteries and all knowledge, and if I have a faith that can move mountains, but do not have love, I am nothing. If I give all I possess to the poor and give over my body to hardship that I may boast, but do not have love, I gain nothing. (1 Corinthians 13:1–3)

Who would want to be a part of a church fellowship where everyone sacrifices their time, energies and money to build up the church, but who are also rude, mean-spirited and unforgiving towards one another? I dare say that Christ would not be pleased or impressed.

Chances are that you are a very compassionate and merciful person to others. When someone hurts you and returns to apologize and asks for your forgiveness, you willingly provide it. My question for you is, are you merciful with yourself? Do you forgive yourself easily? Are you kind to yourself? Do you show yourself grace after you have sinned? Or is it your habit to put yourself into the spiritual doghouse and punish yourself like some kind of spiritual masochist? Is it not possible for you to be gentle with yourself?

Once in a while we will meet a person who is truly gentle, but that is a quality that is difficult to find in a world that esteems toughness. Modern society has very little room for a man who is gentle. Yet that is who Jesus was. In prophesying about the virtues of Christ, Isaiah said this about the Lord's character:

> *He will not quarrel or cry out;*
>   *no one will hear his voice in the streets.*
> *A bruised reed he will not break,*
>   *and a smoldering wick he will not snuff out.*
>
> (Matthew 12:19–20)

Isn't that a beautiful image of Christ? Jesus, of course, had a tough side to him as well, as the religious leaders and Romans clearly experienced, but he was a man who was dressed in gentleness. To the poor woman who was about to be stoned to death for being caught in the act of adultery in John 8, to the lepers, the blind and the deaf whom he healed throughout Scripture, right up to his dying breath with the thief on the cross, Jesus displayed his gentleness. He is gentle to you and me, too. He listens intently, he cares deeply, he touches our lives with kindness and respect, and in doing so does not "break the crushed reed, or snuff the faltering wick" (Isaiah 42:2 NJB).

One of the reasons we are so hard on ourselves after a spiritual fall is because we can mistakenly believe that our previous efforts to change and mature before we acted out in sin have somehow been erased, as if all of the lessons learned no longer existed. That's just not true. As our example, imagine you are in a 20 mile bike race and at the 10 mile marker, you fall off the bike. Would you have to go back to the starting line to begin the race over again? No. You would simply need to pick yourself up, wipe yourself off, and get back on the bike to start racing again at the place where you fell. The ten miles that you had just completed wouldn't have been erased. All of your hard work and effort would still be there. Likewise when we sin. All of your hard work and efforts to mature spiritually prior to acting out in sin is still there. You don't need to start the race over again, you just need to get up, wipe yourself off, accept God's grace, and start riding where you left off.

There is an old quote that says, "The greatest tragedy in life is to have no burden to bear." We all deal with burdens, challenges, suffering and heartache. We all must live with our own faults, errors and sins; however, we can learn from life's difficulties if we let them teach us. But they do not need define us. There is so much more to us than our troubles and weaknesses. Be kind to yourself and learn from your mistakes to do better and to improve, not to punish yourself. If Jesus is willing to forgive you immediately, shouldn't you be able to do the same? Jesus says, in effect, "Mercy is what pleases me, not your sacrifice."

Practice the three steps listed above after you've failed, making them a part of your daily life. Don't let yourself nosedive; there's no need to let a bad few minutes turn into a bad day. Love the way God smells; in your repentance, pray as soon as you recognize that you've sinned and return to the Lord's loving grasp as fast as possible. Be merciful with yourself; don't waste your time punishing yourself. That's a losing game, all day long. Treat yourself the way Christ treats you, with kindness, gentleness and respect. Living daily with these routines will help ensure that you will not "crash the plane" but rather, like the toddler in France who fell seven stories into the arms of a doctor, allow you to bounce safely into the arms of Christ.

Small Group Discussion Questions

1. If you really believe that "perfection is not the goal, but faithfulness is," how will this affect the way you respond to sin and failure in your life and in the lives of others?

2. In what ways does the practicing of an athlete relate to your journey of becoming Christlike?

3. How can we grab hold of the "yoke" of Jesus to help pull us out of a spiritual nosedive?

4. Jesus says, "Go and learn what this means: 'I desire mercy, not sacrifice.' For I have not come to call the righteous, but sinners." What does this mean to you?

5. What is a favorite scripture of yours that helps you, when dealing with failure, to "fail well" and bounce back into the arms of Christ?

6. How has this book helped you most in the way you look at and face temptations and challenges in your life?

End Notes:

1. Fraser, Christian. "Paris baby 'survives six-storey fall unharmed'" BBC News. 2 Nov. 2010. http://www.bbc.com/news/world-europe-11673774.

2. Ibid.

3. Dillner, Luisa. "How did a baby survive a plane crash that killed 100 people?" *The Guardian*. The Guardian News. 15 July 2003. http://www.theguardian.com/lifeandstyle/2003/jul/15/healthandwellbeing.health1.

4. "'Miracle baby' survives 11-story fall from apartment window in Minnesota." *The Telegraph*. Telegraph Media Group. 15 May 2014. http://www.telegraph.co.uk/news/worldnews/northamerica/usa/10832517/Miracle-baby-survives-11-story-fall-from-apartment-window-in-Minnesota.html.

5. Nouwen, Henri J.M. *The Inner Voice of Love*. New York: Image Doubleday, 1996. Print.

Chapter Nine

Quitting Lasts Forever

Age wrinkles the body. Quitting wrinkles the soul. —Samuel Ullman

Harriet Beecher Stowe, the great American abolitionist and author of *Uncle Tom's Cabin*, knew more than a little about not giving up in the midst of intense struggle. She once wrote, "When you get into a tight place and everything goes against you, till it seems as though you could not hang on a minute longer, never give up, for that is just the place and time that the tide will turn." Theodore Roosevelt said, "Far better it is to dare mighty things, to win glorious triumphs, even though checkered by failure, than to rank with those poor spirits who neither enjoy much nor suffer much, because they live in a gray twilight that knows neither victory nor defeat."

And herein lies one of the greatest challenges in our world today. We live in an environment and culture that says that quitting is fine, a viable option, and this outlook can easily filter into our attitudes towards our Christian faith. Certainly there are situations in life when quitting something you started is necessary or at the very least inconsequential in the overall schematic of your life. That being said, we are surrounded by an overabundance of examples of how people of all ages find it too easy to quit at almost anything that is inconvenient or even hints at being difficult.

A study with nearly 50,000 participants, conducted by Brown University's School of Medicine, Brandeis University, National Children's Medical Center and New England Center for Pediatric Psychology, found that in the United States, at least thirty-six percent of school-aged children will not attempt a difficult or strenuous task. Furthermore, parents report that these children will quit tasks that are challenging "most or all of the time."[1]

Any parent who ever put their child into competitive sports in their local community has no doubt heard the whine, "I want to quit," once the child was required to get up early on a Saturday morning for practice. In my opinion, any parent worth their salt has responded, "No way! Get your behind out of that bed; you'll finish what you started and you will have fun doing it, whether you like it or not!" (See why my kids love me so much?) According to the National Alliance for Sports, however, the majority of parents would not agree with my method of childrearing. Studies show that seventy percent of children quit playing league sports by age thirteen and never play again; and nearly half that number quit mid-season![2]

Let's move on to situations in life where quitting carries significantly greater consequences. In my home nation of Canada, in 2008, the government projected that a stunning 40.7 percent of marriages would end in divorce before the thirtieth wedding anniversary.[3] In the United States, 8,300 high school students drop out of school each day (yes, you read that right, each and every day!).[4] And according to the U.S. Department of Education, 25 percent of students will not graduate from high school.[5] As reported by Forbes Magazine, 2 million Americans quit their job every month. The reason given by 31 percent of them is that they didn't like their boss, another 31 percent did so because of a lack of empowerment, 35 percent due to internal politics and 43 percent because of a lack of recognition.[6] Now, granted, some had perfectly legitimate reasons why they quit their jobs or saw divorce as a necessary step in their lives, and I want to be careful not to paint everyone with the same broad brush, but taking this caution into account, you don't have to look very hard to see that we live in a culture that says, "When the going gets tough, quitting is a viable option."

Do you recall the examples I provided in Chapter One when discussing those who excelled and became superstars: Hank Aaron, Warren Buffett, Julia Child and Michael Jordan? When it comes to the likes of these icons, we must ask what separates these people who were great in their respective fields from those who were just average. Surely one of the qualities was their absolute refusal to quit, their dogged determination to push through pain, adversity, difficulty and criticism. They kept practicing, studying, trying and learning long after everyone else had gone home. Granted, this can't be the only ingredient to their phenomenal achievements. Certainly there has to be more to it than that, like talent, for instance, but can we not agree that those who triumph over anything significant in life, regardless in what arena, do so in large part because of an absolute refusal to surrender, regardless of how many times they have failed in the attempt?

Calvin Coolidge said:

> Nothing in the world can take the place of persistence. Talent will not; nothing is more common than unsuccessful men with talent. Genius will not; unrewarded genius is almost a proverb. Education will not; the world is full of educated derelicts. Persistence and determination alone are omnipotent.

Paul says the same thing, only more succinctly, in Galatians 6:9: "Let us not become wearing in doing good, for at the proper time we will reap a harvest if we do not give up."

When It Comes My Time to Go

When I was a young minister, just starting out, there was a Christian man in my congregation who was born with cerebral palsy, which left him quadriplegic and confined to a wheelchair all of his sixty years. His name was Larry Wigle. To say that Larry lived a challenging life would be a gross understatement. Due to this incredibly debilitating disease, Larry had to go through day-to-day challenges that few of us could appreciate. Imagine, if you can, what it would be like to have to have someone get you out of bed and dress you, or undress you and put you to bed every day for sixty years. Think of the challenges involved in having others bathe you, or what it must have been like to be confined to a wheelchair every waking moment of your life. Yet with all of these difficulties, Larry's tenacious character and his perseverance, along with his tough determination to survive, pushed him to do great things with his life.

For instance, Larry worked for a Canadian government agency called Employment Canada as the manager of their Employment Equity Program. During his years there, Larry was dedicated to making the lives of the handicapped easier within Canadian society. Much of the legislation in this area that has been passed in Canada is due to the direct influence of Larry and the recommendations that he made.

As impressive as those accomplishments are, however, Larry's greatest triumph in life was when he gave his life to Jesus and became a Christian. This did not occur until he was in his mid-fifties, but those final years of his life were dedicated to Christ. Because he was so moved by the cross, Larry soared as a Christian. Only under the most difficult circumstances did he ever miss meetings of the body. He loved the church. He was happiest when he was able to fellowship with other Christians.

I remember Sunday services in the middle of winter when we were in the middle of a blizzard and because the snow was so deep, many members didn't come to service for safety concerns, and yet, there would be Larry, in his motorized wheelchair, singing and praising God. I would think, "How on earth did he get here in that snowstorm?" He constantly brought friends to church, was always sacrificial and had a deep love for the word of God. As his pastor and friend, I will always remember him as an example of a faithful Christian man who lived with courage and commitment and a standard in which he refused to complain or fall back on excuses, regardless of the challenges that he faced.

A few years after becoming a Christian, Larry became quite ill and was hospitalized with congestive heart disease. The day before he died, I sat with him and discussed the funeral arrangements, but then, knowing that his time was short and wanting Larry to spend his final hours in peace, I asked if there was anything he wanted to confess or get off his chest before meeting the Lord.

Larry didn't have much strength left, but he was able to whisper to me words that I have never forgotten. He simply said: "Guy, my conscious is clear. I have nothing to confess; I am ready to meet God." As tears welled up in my eyes and I held his hand, I started to pull away, thinking he had finished his statement, but then he looked up at me and pulled me closer and said, with a bit of a smile on his face, "And oh, yeah, it's been great to have been a part of Jesus' church." Larry Wigle passed away and met his Maker a few hours later.

When it comes my time to pass over to the other side, I want to go like Larry did, with a clear conscience, nothing to confess, grateful for having been in Jesus' church and ready to meet my God.

I love stories like Larry's, because it speaks of one's refusal to live the life of a victim, of one who refused to swim in an ocean of self-pity when the circumstances were incredibly difficult. Larry could have used his illness to move towards despair and victimhood, but instead, he chose to rise above that to move his life towards helping others. Over and over again, Larry kept returning to the Lord and trusting in his love and strength to make it to the end victoriously.

As I said earlier in this chapter, I fear we live in a society today in which many feel like they are entitled to an easy life or good treatment. The truth is, they are neither entitled nor not entitled to those things. Life happens. As Christians, it's not whether or not life is easy or hard, it's what we do with whatever circumstance God allows us to be in. Either we will use our situation to bless others and glorify him, or we will not.

I wanted to write this because I've heard too many Christians complain how unfair life is because they suffer with one area of weakness in their life or another, and then blame God as if somehow they were being treated unjustly. All too often, those who live with that attitude have used it as an excuse to stop fighting and go ahead and give in to temptation. Being a same-sex-attracted Christian who counsels other men and women who are as well, it has especially frustrated me how often I hear this from these brothers and sisters in Christ. Listen: whatever your challenge, God is not ashamed of you or embarrassed of you, so stop being ashamed and embarrassed of yourself. God has given you many incredible gifts and talents, and you are valuable to him. Go do something great with your life and refuse to allow this area of weakness to define you!

Sadly, and to my shame, I wasted almost two decades of my Christian life drowning in self-pity and feeling like a victim. It's no way to live your life as a follower of Christ. I lost too many years feeling sorry for myself and staying silent, afraid of what others would think, in fact paralyzed, when I could have been helping others. Life may be hard, but before I die, I'm determined to help as many people as possible and glorify God with my life while I do it. I refuse to live my life like a victim and to make excuses why I should go ahead and resign. No way! When it comes my time to die, I want to go out like Larry Wigle did.

Three Critical Lessons from Another Dying Man

A prison cell is hardly a place conducive to the writing of any literary endeavor. Yet, it is a curious historical fact that those in prison have put many of the world's masterpieces to pen while they were behind bars. For example, John Bunyan wrote his immortal *The Pilgrim's Progress* while he languished in jail. *Don Quixote* was written from a Spanish prison cell in the seventeenth century. Sir Walter Raleigh composed his *The History of the World* while he was a prisoner in the Tower of London.

Another example is from the scripture that we are going to read next. The apostle Paul, who towards the end of his life was a prisoner in Rome, wrote no fewer than five books while he was in jail. During his first internment in Rome, Paul produced four letters, namely Ephesians, Colossians, Philippians and Philemon. During his second imprisonment in that same city, he wrote his second letter to his son in the faith, the young preacher Timothy. The interim between Paul's two imprisonments was about four years.

During his first incarceration, the authorities were rather lenient in how they handled the apostle. That is to say that although he was under constant watch by a Roman soldier, he was permitted to reside in his own apartment, which means Paul was under house arrest and was allowed the additional privilege of having visitors. But during his second jail term it was a very different story. This time, he was not so moderately dealt with. Indeed, to use his own words, "...for which I am suffering even to the point of being chained like a criminal" (2 Timothy 2:9), which is to say that he was cast into a filthy, maximum-security Roman penitentiary.

Early historians have left us descriptions of the Roman dungeons of Paul's day, and it isn't a pretty picture they paint. The typical cell was completely devoid of any hygienic facilities whatsoever. The hole that Paul would be writing the book of 2 Timothy from was tiny and cramped. The cell had little light, no heat and was no doubt foul smelling. Rats, lice and everything in between overran the dirty little cubicle. It was in such a hole as that that the apostle Paul was thrown and wrote his second letter to Timothy.

Perhaps we can see him, in our mind's eye, as he sits there in a corner of the tiny, unclean cage. He is in chains; several weeks' growth of stubble on his face, he looks haggard and unkempt, and his hair is grey, for he is an old man now. He is huddled over the small candle that lights his page as he takes up his pen to write, long into the night, to his friend Timothy. He begins to author his final goodbye, as these are the last words we have recorded of this man, for in a short time, he will be executed. Listen to the words of him who had suffered so much for the cause of Christ, who had been so violently mistreated and abused, who so courageously shared his faith and his life to save as many as possible and whose end is now upon him.

What can we learn from a dying man, just before he is executed, that will help us in our times of struggle and weakness? There are three lessons in 2 Timothy 4:9–18 that I want to call our attention to that if we would just implement, would assist us in never quitting, regardless of the extreme nature of our difficulties.

As for me, my life has already been poured out as an offering to God. **The time of my death is near. I have fought the good fight, I have finished the race, and I have remained faithful.** *And now the prize awaits me—the crown of righteousness, which the Lord, the righteous Judge, will give me on the day of his return. And the prize is not just for me but for all who eagerly look forward to his appearing.*

Timothy, please come as soon as you can. Demas has deserted me because he loves the things of this life and has gone to Thessalonica. Crescens has gone to Galatia, and Titus has gone to Dalmatia. Only Luke is with me. Bring Mark with you when you come, for he will be helpful to me in my ministry. I sent Tychicus to Ephesus. When you come, be sure to bring the coat I left with Carpus at Troas. **Also bring my books, and especially my papers.**

Alexander the coppersmith did me much harm, but the Lord will judge him for what he has done. Be careful of him, for he fought against everything we said.

*The first time I was brought before the judge, no one came with me. Everyone abandoned me. **May it not be counted against them.** But the Lord stood with me and gave me strength so that I might preach the Good News in its entirety for all the Gentiles to hear. And he rescued me from certain death. Yes, and the Lord will deliver me from every evil attack and will bring me safely into his heavenly Kingdom. All glory to God forever and ever! Amen.* (NLT, emphasis added)

The words of a dying man. You can feel his pain and loneliness as he concludes his letter begging Timothy *twice* to hurry and come to him. "Get here soon, Timothy, because I am tired and lonely. Only Doctor Luke is here with me in Rome to encourage me. Other than him, I've been forsaken and left all alone, not by God, but by men. The church here turned their back on me at my first trial, and they certainly aren't falling over themselves trying to help me now. Either the Christians do not know where I am or they do not care, for no one ever comes to see me anymore. Even our friend Demas has left me, loving this world more. On top of all that, Timothy, I am hidden away in obscurity, my whereabouts having been kept such a tight secret by the Roman officials that no one could find me if they wanted to. So get here soon!"

According to *Foxe's Book of Martyrs*, it was not long after Paul wrote this letter that Nero started his savage campaign against Christians, and Paul was taken outside the city and his head cut off. Some of the book seems like he's jumping from one topic to the next, like he's just pouring out his thoughts because he knows his time is near. When a man is writing his final words before he passes off into eternity, he spills his heart. There are a few things we can learn from Paul here, as we close off this chapter.

1. **Stay in the fight.** Tough times don't last, but tough people do. I love how Paul starts with, "The time of my death is near. I have fought a good fight, I have finished the race, and I have remained faithful." Remember his words in 1 Corinthians 9:24–27, "I do not run like someone running aimlessly; I do not fight like a boxer beating

the air. No, I strike a blow to my body and make it my slave so that after I have preached to others, I myself will not be disqualified for the prize." Paul was a kind, compassionate and humble man, but he was no wilting flower. He was a strong man with deep and powerful convictions that kept him faithful to the end.

2. Have a love for the Scriptures. Paul tells Timothy that when he stops off at Troas he needs to pick up Paul's winter coat, his books and especially the parchments. When Paul was on his third missionary journey, he had visited Troas. When the disciples had met there to eat, Paul taught them well past midnight because he knew he would leave the next day. When he departed, he left behind his coat, books and parchments. The parchments would have been portions of the Hebrew Scriptures.[7] Paul was a scholar and Bible lover to the bitter end. Even in prison, where he sat weak and sick and soon to die, he wanted his books to study and show himself approved.

3. Forgive those who have hurt you. Like Jesus, Paul spent most of his life serving others. But here we find him in his most distraught moment in life, at a time when he no doubt needed someone to stand by his side and serve him, and sadly, there was no one. "The first time I was brought before the judge, no one was with me. Everyone had abandoned me. I hope it will not be counted against them" (2 Timothy 4:16 NLT).

If you or I were in Paul's position, can you imagine the dejection, the loneliness, the complete isolation and the bitterness that would want to swell up in our heart? Maybe, somewhere in his journeys, he had come across Matthew's written account of Jesus' life and read these words: "But if you do not forgive others their sins, your Father will not forgive your sins" (Matthew 6:15).

So we see Paul imitating the heart of Jesus, and in his most distressed moment, he becomes more like Christ in this act than in any other that he had previously carried out. For just as Jesus begged, "Father, forgive them, for they do not know what they are doing" (Luke 23:34), Paul in his final moments says, "I hope it will not be counted against them."

When Stephen was being stoned to death, before he breathed his last, he imitated Jesus as well and cried, "Lord, do not hold this sin against them" (Acts 7:60). There is nothing so lovely and nothing so rare as true forgiveness. When an unforgiving spirit is threatening to turn our hearts to bitterness, we need to stop and hear again our Lord asking forgiveness for those who were killing him. We need to imitate Paul and Stephen as they imitated their Lord.

Too often Christians leave the faith because someone in the church, who should have known better, said or did something to cause hurt and damage. Never give anyone or any circumstance so much power over your life that it would propel you to turn your back on Christ.

Paul was able to make it to the end faithfully because he was tough and refused to make excuses for the difficulties he faced, because he loved the Scriptures, and finally because he lived striving to forgive those who offended him. These are the ingredients that make up a faithful life. My friend Larry Wigle refused to quit in spite of his extraordinary circumstances and struggles, and he took his strength from the love he had for the church and his worship of God. Quit at sports, OK. Let's face it, you probably weren't that good anyway. Quit that hobby you started, all right; all those dumb baseball cards were doing nothing but sitting in binders collecting dust. Sell your collection for twenty bucks and move on. Quit your job, whatever; find a new one. Quit school, well, not a good choice in my estimation, but you'll survive (not well, probably, but it won't be the end of the world). Quit on Christ and the church? Never. That kind of quitting lasts forever. It simply cannot be a choice in your mind, not ever. The eternal consequences of such a decision make it so that the option has to be completely eradicated from your thinking.

As the years pass in my Christian life I become more and more convinced that Christianity is not for wimps. Wimps are people who run away at the first sign of trouble. Christianity is for a special breed of men and women, those of a particular metal, people of the sort who, come "hell or high water," will not quit. Christianity is for men and women who are resolutely determined to be around at the finish and who have made up their minds to smile through their earthly tears even though the journey at times may seem long. It is for these individuals that heaven was made.

Small Group Discussion Questions

1. "Nothing in the world can take the place of persistence." When are you most tempted to quit?

2. How have you let your weaknesses define you?

3. How is entitlement revealed in the way you respond when life is hard or unfair?

4. How does forgiveness set us free from the bondage of feeling the victim?

5. What decisions can you make today that will ensure that you fight the good fight until the end, never quitting or giving up?

End Notes:

1. Jackson, Rebecca. "How Not to Raise a Generation of Quitters." Psychology Today. 17 Aug. 2014. https://www.psychologytoday.com/blog/school-thought/201408/how-not-raise-generation-quitters.

2. Dillworth, Kate. "Would You Let Your Child Quit a Sport in Mid-Season?" National Alliance for Youth Sports. 2 July 2014. http://www.nays.org/blog/would-you-let-your-child-quit-a-sport-mid-season/.

3. "Family Life - Divorce." Indicators of Well-being in Canada. Employment and Social Development Canada. 29 Dec. 2014. http://www4.hrsdc.gc.ca/.3ndic.1t.4r@-eng.jsp?iid=76.

4. "High School Dropout Statistics." Education Week, Children Trends Database. Statistic Brain Research Institute. 17 Mar. 2015. http://www.statisticbrain.com/high-school-dropout-statistics/.

5. Swanson, Christopher B. "U.S. Graduation Rate Continues Decline." Graduation by the Numbers. Education Week. 2 June 2010. http://www.edweek.org/ew/articles/2010/06/10/34swanson.h29.html.

6. Hall, Allan. "'I'm Outta Here!' Why 2 Million Americans Quit Every Month (And 5 Steps to Turn the Epidemic Around)." Forbes. 11 Mar. 2013. http://www.forbes.com/sites/alanhall/2013/03/11/im-outta-here-why-2-million-americans-quit-every-month-and-5-steps-to-turn-the-epidemic-around/.

7. "2 Timothy 4:13." Expositor's Greek Testament. N.d. http://biblehub.com/commentaries/2_timothy/4-13.htm.

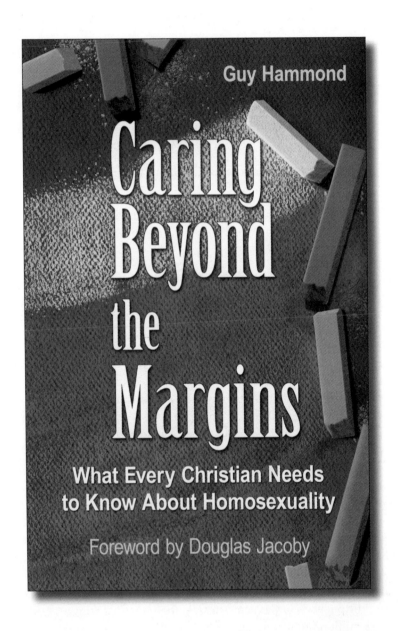

Guy Hammond

Caring Beyond the Margins

What Every Christian Needs to Know About Homosexuality

Foreword by Douglas Jacoby

Also available from www.ipibooks.com

www.StrengthInWeakness.org

www.ipibooks.com